Edited by A

MW01481886

Be *you* Unapologetically

Love and Lead from the Heart!

AMANDA DA SILVA

Copyright © 2022 by Amanda Da Silva

All rights reserved.

It is not legal to reproduce, duplicate, or transmit any part of
this document in either electronic means or printed format. Recording of
this publication is strictly prohibited.

Editor: Andreia McLean
getinviting.com

Book Design: Devon Adamson
@devadamson

Published by Ho'ola Publishing
hoolapublishing.com

First Printing: August 2022

For more support in living your dream life, check out:
www.amanda-dasilva.com and www.dseducationgroup.com

ho'ola
PUBLISHING

To my dear Momma, Heather, who for 44 years has always been there to support, encourage, and console, when necessary, as I strove to achieve a purposeful life full of joy, happiness, and fulfillment. Mom, I love you! Thank you for always believing in me.

To my loving husband, Carlos, and my wonderful boys Jacob, Jaden, and Jordan, you're my raison d'être. I love you profoundly, with all my heart, and I hope this book inspires you to pursue the things that excite you the most. Live, love, and serve in this lifetime to the fullest! Infuse gratitude into your daily life—the world is a beautiful place.

To my extended family, your life stories and experiences inspire me to commit myself to support and empower others. You're my family, always. This is for you!

And finally, a special dedication to my fur babies Bailey, Cocoa, Taffy, the late Kahlua, hamster Twinkle, and birds, Snowflake and Amelia. XOX

FORWARD

Mindset, leadership, resilience, and growth… Amanda Da Silva projects the kind of enthusiasm and encouragement that drives everyone around her to show up and want to be better. When we as individuals – whether business owners, or family members, or participants in a community – invest in ourselves, we strengthen that community and the effects of our work come back tenfold. What Amanda Da Silva provides in the pages to follow isn't the kind of book you read once and put away. This is a guide to visit and revisit as you grow into your fullest self.

As an entrepreneur and multi-business owner, finding a balance between my personal and professional life is a constant endeavour. My entrepreneurial journey certainly hasn't been a straight path lit with arrows and clear signs on the path to success. There have been moments when I wanted to give up the responsibility and weight of carrying my own future, and the future of my family, on my shoulders. In those moments, I turn to my inspiration – my why. I remember that it's my leadership, creativity, and resilience that propel me and inspire them. Remembering this fills me with determination and the strength to forge forward with renewed enthusiasm.

When life feels like a gruelling journey or like an endless uphill battle, learning to Love and Lead from the Heart will fill your cup and turn a difficult moment into the most gratifying of adventures. Starting right now in this moment, you've picked up this book and decided to start on the path to living unapologetically. Think of how incredible it will feel to step into that version of yourself – what an amazing way to start. I am excited for you to ~~read~~ thrive!

Shelly Lynn Hughes

Shelly Lynn Hughes
Founder & Creator Pursuit:365
& CEO of Fresh Magazine

CONTENTS

INTRODUCTION

Do you often find yourself striving to find that perfect balance between your professional and personal life?

Are you actively seeking to become the best version of yourself?

Perhaps you're looking for the right tools to unlock your full potential and reach optimal success.

Imagine what your life would be like if you were entirely emboldened to be unapologetically you and show up as your most vibrant self.

If you picked up this book, you most likely believe in living an unapologetic life. You don't need to be convinced of the power of loving and leading from the heart. Be You Unapologetically resides in this collective understanding and offers you not only the why but the how to love and lead from the heart as your most authentic self. This book is meant to help you as a leader to master your inner "self," cultivate confidence, embark on your journey of self-actualization, and find your purpose, but also guide others on their own paths to success.

My mission has always been to contribute to the creation of a more caring, morally just, judgment-free, and genuinely appreciative society. More importantly, one that has the right skill set and empathy to make the collective of humanity better and stronger together.

This book engages every aspect of our lives: from feeling stuck and unproductive, to developing the right mindset, to thinking from a place of abundance rather than scarcity, to challenging our self-limiting beliefs and building emotional resilience.

I designed this guide to help women who find themselves in a position similar to mine. We're constantly told our value and worth stem from our productivity and how much we contribute, so it's hard to detach ourselves from that state of mind. This often leads to feelings of frustration and burnout.

Not only that, but we're also conditioned to think that suppressing our feelings and emotions is our best bet for being taken more seriously. This makes it incredibly difficult to face obstacles and setbacks, especially when we feel so disinclined to ask for help.

But things don't have to be this way, and they shouldn't either!

This book will help you realize that there is strength in vulnerability and that weakness doesn't come from showing compassion to others and ourselves; rather, it comes from a place of fear and judgment.

This book is meant to take you on a journey of sorts—a challenging one perhaps, but a rewarding one, nonetheless. The end goal is to establish a healthier perception of yourself, one that doesn't involve loathing, anger, and resentment. The most powerful antidotes to these negative feelings are mindful acceptance, kindness, and compassion.

In addition, this book is meant to bring you comfort in knowing that there's no shame or guilt to be felt in a position of leadership. Often, people assume that leaders love their status because of the power they have. But we all know that true leadership is enjoying the meaningful and purposeful impact you are capable of creating— and the positive change you can bring to the lives of those around you.

When you detach yourself from all the deeply rooted fears, worries, and anxieties, you're also freeing up space for you to discover your true values and the things that matter to you the most. Because at the end of the day, it's these things that will guide you forward into the life you want to live, but also help you guide others on their own paths.

As that space continues to expand, you will learn how to redirect your energy and focus toward the people and experiences that allow you to grow, spread your wings, and free yourself from the shackles and constraints of your past.

So, are you ready to embark on this journey?

xox

Amanda Da Silva

Pessimism becomes a self-fulfilling prophecy; it reproduces itself by crippling our willingness to act.

- Howard Zinn

Then she told herself to stop her nonsense. If you looked for things to make you feel hurt and wretched and unnecessary, you were certain to find them, more easily each time, so easily, soon, that you did not even realize you had gone out searching.

- Dorothy Parker

Most of us don't fear that we are not enough; what most of us really fear is our own greatness. Most of us have a fear of success. Why? Because we don't think that we deserve to be successful in anything. This is why people recklessly spend their money or don't work as hard as they could or do things that they know are wrong. They are hindering their own success on purpose because they don't think they deserve it. They cut their own legs out from underneath them on purpose. They are self-sabotaging.

- Lisa Bedrick

Do the best you can until you know better. Then when you know better; do better.

- Maya Angelou

BEWARE OF SELF-FULFILLING PROPHECIES

A self-fulfilling prophecy is a socio-psychological term used to describe when a prediction causes itself to become true. A self-imposed self-fulfilling prophecy is a phenomenon that occurs when your own expectations influence your actions and results in the expected (often feared or negative) conclusion. Understanding self-fulfilling prophecies can help us not only to avoid them but to wield them for good.

Our whole lives, we've been conditioned to dread "worst-case scenarios," to do everything we can to avoid facing difficulties, to run away from conflict, to withdraw from confrontation, and to deflect bad situations to the best of our ability.

We know obstacles and challenges are a ubiquitous part of life, but we always secretly hope to preserve the integrity of our bubble. We sigh out of relief at the end of each day that we managed to completely avert a catastrophe. Yet the unshakable feeling that this stream of "good days" is eventually going to come to a stop lingers in the back of our minds.

Despite how many times you try to suppress that tiny voice, it still manages to come to the surface, often inviting a wave of fear and uncertainty with it, "this is too good to be true, too good to last. . ." So, we anticipate the worst with paralyzing horror.

Then when it does happen, and we come across difficult times, we're not sure whether to take solace in the fact that we were right or whether we should resent the universe for our "luck." So, you have to ask yourself, "Would I rather be right, or would I rather be happy?"

Beware of self-fulfilling prophecies because they come true.

When all we can think about are our fears and worries, we can find ourselves constantly overwhelmed and on the brink of a breakdown. Those negative thoughts and assumptions occupy so much space in our heads that there's no room left for much else.

We're exhausted from dealing with our spiraling thoughts throughout the day. As a result, we are unable to live in the moment or appreciate the present for what it is. We're always thinking about what could go wrong in a given situation and how that negative outcome will somehow be our fault.

The truth is, our brains are very much like computer programs, in the sense that whatever we program them to do, they will do. When we keep telling ourselves things like, "I make everything worse," "it all went wrong because of me," "I will never be enough," or "I'm not as smart as other people think I am," we're also conditioning our brains to assimilate that information.

In this way, when things go the way we expected them to, our self-limiting beliefs become a self-fulfilling prophecy. What we think is what we get.

This is a chain reaction called TFAR: our thoughts dictate our feelings which in turn influence our actions, then leading to results.

And because our results reinforce our initial thoughts, after proving ourselves right over and over again, these thoughts become beliefs, hence the self-fulfilling prophecy aspect.

The thing is, a lot of us are aware of this reality. We know our self-limiting beliefs plague us in some capacity. We're conscious of our negative self-talk. And we realize the power those thoughts have on us and how much of an impact they make on our lives.

Yet we're convinced that's how things should be because we know no other way and because that's the only mindset we're familiar with, so venturing into the unknown can be scary. Sometimes, despite how miserable we are, we cling to that misery because of how familiar it feels, because being right feels like a safer bet than being happy. We've grown accustomed to it so much that it becomes a safety blanket.

Other times we refuse to let go because this mindset becomes entrenched in who we are as a part of our identity, and we're afraid there isn't much else beyond it—that if we set it free, we won't be able to recognize ourselves. That is a scary thought, but a dangerous one as well, because of the power it yields. This is what makes us feel stuck, unable to move forward, but unable to regress either.

We keep analyzing every possible pathway, weighing the risks and rewards of every potential decision, putting every little detail under scrutiny, yet when it comes to making the leap, we're completely frozen.

On some occasions, because we spent too much time thinking and overthinking every element, we often find that we've missed the opportunity to act and the window to take a stand, so we mourn that loss, and we retreat back to the safety of our worn-out minds.

Then, to punish ourselves for our shortcomings or "laziness," we begin to overcompensate. "I took a longer break today, so I need to work harder tomorrow," "I had a cheat meal for lunch, so I need to work out for an extra hour," "I was ten minutes late to work, so I need to stay overtime to show my commitment and dedication," "I had a self-care day yesterday, so I can't have another one until next week," . . . sound familiar?

We keep pushing all these rules on ourselves, repeatedly feeding our brains that everything comes with a price, that we can't relax if we didn't earn it, that we can't afford to sit in a bath for 45 minutes while reading a book or listening to music, that we don't deserve to just sit and do nothing for more than 30 seconds, that we have to be working at all times, and if we're not then we need to guilt-trip ourselves into it, that we need to be more productive, more efficient, more valuable, more useful, that our entire self-worth rests on how many tasks we've accomplished that day and how many objectives we've reached.

So, we drain our coffee machines one cup at a time, we drain our brains one task at a time, and we drain our willingness to keep fighting one battle at a time. Part of the problem is the toxic culture we live in that glorifies being constantly busy, constantly burning the midnight oil, and constantly overworking ourselves to exertion, as if without the work we do and the contribution we make, we amount to nothing. It sounds heavy but familiar. And there's more.

The other part of the problem is that we've internalized that phobia of relaxing, taking time for ourselves when we need it, listening to our bodies' needs, and knowing when to stop and when to push back.

We have to make a thousand engagements, overbook ourselves, overextend ourselves, overcommit, overfill our schedules, every hour, minute, and second accounted for, until we're left with nothing, no time to think, no time to breathe, no time to exist.

We exist through our work, through our goals, through our accomplishments; that's our only legacy. And then we get the occasional reminder to "indulge" in more self-care practices, so we can salvage whatever parts are left from our burned-out selves and amass the energy to keep going.

And we indulge as if taking time for ourselves was a luxury that only this elite club of overachievers and perfectionists has access to. Then we're instantly filled with the guilt and shame of allowing ourselves to sit back and unwind. But even during what is supposed to be a self-care day, we can't silence that tiny voice in the back of our head telling us we should be working, we should be doing something, we can't afford downtime, as it will only slow us down.

It's hard to relax when all you can think about are the piles and stacks of work you have to get done. You try to be in the present moment and focus on yourself, but at the same time, you can't think of anything else but work.

You're not resting, yet you're not getting anything done either. You feel even guiltier for having wasted a whole day stressing over what you should be doing.

This is, in part, due to your mindset but also to your emotional fitness. You're most likely feeling stuck in a guilt cycle that has become almost second nature to your mind, accompanying you wherever you go, leeching onto your every thought.

There is a light at the end of the tunnel. There are methods and tools you can use to shift these negative self-limiting beliefs that perpetuate negative self-fulfilling prophecies. You can flip the script so you generate positive prophecies for yourself and your life. If all this is true about negative self-talk there's reason to believe power exists in positive self-talk too. What if we cultivated that? What if you had the exact tools you needed to talk yourself into the life you want?

In the following chapters, we will dig deeper into the mindset and the self, so you can gain an accurate insight into how they operate and how you can make the transition to a more fulfilling, abundant, and positive life.

CHAPTER ONE RECAP:

It can feel easier to sit in the smug feeling of being "right" about the bad things that happen because we "knew they were coming" rather than learn to anticipate and invite positivity into our lives.

We have a culture that perpetuates a phobia of relaxing, so "not busy" = "lazy" becomes the script we feed ourselves.

Strength in mindfulness, resilience, and emotional fitness can all contribute to breaking a negative cycle and reversing self-fulfilling prophecies.

PUT IT INTO ACTION:

"Our actions ripple beyond our comprehension."

SIMPLE AFFIRMATION CHALLENGE

Duration: 5 days

Opportunity: Every morning for 5 days, first thing in the morning before you start your day, sit or stand in front of a mirror, look yourself in the eyes and repeat this simple affirmation: **"Everything is happening around me, and I am truly taken care of."** At the end of Day 5, note how you feel and write it down. Let yourself explore how cultivating this affirmation transforms the way you show up in your day and for yourself!

5-DAY "OPEN TO OPPORTUNITY EXPERIMENT"

Duration: 5 days

Opportunity:

   Step 1: Every morning for 5 days, before you start your day, sit or stand in front of a mirror, look yourself in the eyes and repeat this simple affirmation: "Everything is happening around me, and I am truly taken care of." [option to create your own affirmation—examples in the back of this book!]

   Step 2: Around lunchtime or just after (whatever time is a moment reserved just for you) take 5 minutes to sit in silence and focus on your breath. You don't need to quiet your mind, just let your thoughts roam, but no screens, no sounds other than what's going on around you. Just five minutes. You can do it!

Step 3: Each evening for the 5 days, right before you go to sleep, write down or say aloud one thing you're grateful for that happened that day. It can be simple or complex; you can say it to yourself or to a family member or partner, just make sure it is expressed and not left as a thought in your head. Get it out into the Universe.

Reflect: When you wake up on Day 6, reflect on your energy levels, your mindset, and your happiness over the past few days. How did it feel to let your mind breathe and give yourself space to invite gratefulness into your daily routine? Did you perpetuate any positive self-fulfilling prophecies?

For my Meditation Guide: Powerful Best Practices for Total Alignment of Your Mind, Body, and Soul check out:

www.amanda-dasilva.com/meditation-guide

Notes

We do not see things as they are, we see them as we are.

- *Anaïs Nin*

Learning too soon our limitations, we never learn our powers.

- *Mignon McLaughlin*

Courage is your natural setting. You do not need to become courageous, but rather peel back the layers of self-protective, limiting beliefs that keep you small.

- *Vironika Tugaleva*

If you expect the battle to be insurmountable, you've met the enemy. It's you.

- *Khang Kijarro Nguyen*

CHANGE YOUR MINDSET

Our beliefs give us the power to take action and help us create the roadmap we need to achieve our goals. These same beliefs are also capable of setting us back and preventing us from reaching our full potential. The challenge is most of our beliefs are based on subjective generalizations about our past and biased interpretations of both painful and pleasurable experiences.

Often, we're unconscious of how those beliefs affect our lives and the decisions we make. The limiting ones can cause us to miss out on incredible opportunities. The empowering ones can drive us toward the future of our dreams. Ask yourself, "What is something that I've always wanted to accomplish and haven't? Why haven't I?".

Whatever that reason might be, there will be a self-limiting belief behind it. To disempower old beliefs and replace them, you have to first build awareness of your mindset and attitude. In this chapter, we dissect the five mindset myths holding you back and how you can overcome these self-limiting beliefs to find more happiness and balance.

Myth #1: Adversity Means Regression

When we go through challenging times, we're often blindsided by the swarm of negative emotions and feelings. So much so that it becomes impossible to find the silver lining in a situation we deem worthy of a fight or flight response. So, we let our worries, anxieties, and fears take the wheel as we spiral down into the rabbit hole.

It's completely normal to feel sad, angry, or even unmotivated when facing a difficult situation. Allowing yourself enough time to process, think, and regain your strength is great. However, when you dwell too long on setbacks, you begin to redirect the blame toward yourself, and that's when you're derailing.

Adversity happens. It's an inherent part of life, and I am not going to tell you to shake it off and move on. We all go about things at our own pace, so just because someone else can get back up on their feet quicker than you can, it doesn't make your feelings and emotions less valid.

But before you retreat to self-doubt and defeatism, take a step back to examine if what you think is factual. We often create certain "facts" just because they align with the realities of our lives. We'd rather the knowledge we have of who we are to be true than recognize, for once, that everything is not our fault. Instead of emphasizing every way in which you think you failed, ask yourself, "What can I learn from this?".

A big part of cultivating a growth mindset is seeing adversity as an opportunity for positive change and development, not as an obstacle or a setback. Experiencing adversity allows you to challenge the validity of your beliefs and better understand how much control you have over your day-to-day life.

Often, the takeaway from many situations is that you're responsible for your feelings and your feelings only. You can't control how others react, what they think, or the way they behave. Admitting that and acknowledging it can be incredibly freeing.

With that said, you don't have to enjoy going through tough times to appreciate what knowledge they can impart to you. But if you can build your awareness to learn from them, you can also use it to grow and evolve.

Myth #2: Vulnerability Is a Weakness

A lot of people tend to associate vulnerability with weakness. As women, we struggle with this more than we'd like to admit. We've been taught that for others to take us seriously, we cannot show weakness, and we cannot be vulnerable.

Women have learned to always brace this strong facade and stand our ground like an impenetrable fortress. That we have to build walls and fences to prevent others from peeking in. Even our idea of what makes a strong independent woman is confusingly warped.

We believe that for us to be independent, we can't allow others the knowledge that we have weaknesses, we can't accept help from anybody, and we shouldn't even need help in the first place. Every morning, we put on our clunky armour, and we drag ourselves through the world.

We feel the burdensome load of that metal sheath with every step, yet we refuse to take it off, even for the time it takes to catch our breath. We wear it like a stubborn second skin that won't shed. But the truth is, sometimes just because you can do it yourself doesn't mean you have to.

It's okay to be vulnerable, to accept the help and support of the people in your life, to open up and be heard, be seen, for who you are, rather than what you can do. When you feel vulnerable, you also tend to feel uncomfortable and reluctant to expose your emotional self.

Every instinct you have tells you to close off, put your armour back on, and protect yourself from the outside world. It's also the same feeling you have when you're forced to step out of your comfort zone and do something unfamiliar that compels you to relinquish your control.

When you're not willing to detach yourself from your armour, you can't fully experience your surroundings. The thoughts, feelings, and behaviours you use as a shield not only intercept the 'bad' from getting to you but also prevent you from experiencing the 'good'.

When you allow yourself to be more vulnerable and let your emotions come to the surface, you're also opening up to new ways of doing things and new ways of being. This vulnerability can be incredibly rewarding and can help you build deeper connections with the people in your life.

It also allows room for innovation, creativity, and change. By embracing your authentic self, you stop giving power to what other people think, and focus, instead, on the things that matter to you the most. And the less you hold yourself to impossible ideals of perfection, the easier it will be to stay inspired and keep going.

Myth #3: I Am What I Think

We're often victims of our own constructs. We condition ourselves to feel, think, and live a certain way just because that pattern of being goes with the beliefs we hold. Our perception of ourselves depends on what we wake up thinking that day.

One morning you're energized, motivated, and invincible. The next, you're tired, irritated, and worn out. You wake up on the wrong side of the bed, you have a bad day. You wake up on the right side, you conquer the world . . . Right? Wrong!

One negative feeling, one negative comment, one negative occurrence shouldn't dictate the course of your day. You're not a passive agent in your life, and you shouldn't end up where the current takes you. You control the current, you control the flow, you take yourself where you want to end up.

Granted, you don't have much say on what the people around you think or do, but you have the power to decide how that affects you. Your beliefs influence your thoughts, your thoughts influence your feelings, and your feelings influence your behaviour. It's a simple equation, isn't it? This means if you want to change the quality of your life, first, you need to change your long-held beliefs and attitudes.

The convictions we have about ourselves, others, and the world shape everything from our perception of life to the decisions we make. So when we react out of fear, anger, or frustration, it's harder to discern negative self-talk from our genuine selves.

Then when we suddenly snap at someone, react in a negative way, or make a mistake, we immediately villainize ourselves. But the important thing to consider here is that one misstep or unexpected blunder doesn't make you a bad person. It doesn't suddenly realize all of your dreaded fears about yourself.

No matter what you tell yourself, you are not your thoughts, and you are not your self-limiting beliefs! It takes a lot of courage, patience, and self-compassion to reframe how we're really feeling, identify our negative thoughts for what they are, challenge them, and create positive responses free of judgment and self-doubt.

So you have to take that first step and express a willingness to be more forgiving toward yourself. Only then will true change commence. Only then will your self-limiting beliefs waver and break.

Myth #4: If I'm Not Good at It, I Never Will Be

Throughout our lives, we navigate the world using two different mindsets that define our perceptions of our own abilities: a fixed mindset and a growth mindset. In a fixed mindset, we're convinced that the qualities we have are inherent. They can't be changed, developed, or improved.

Often, with a fixed mindset, we tend to focus on and amplify the qualities and aptitudes we lack rather than those in our possession. Because of that, we're constantly hung up on how we will never be good enough at this thing or the other, that innate talent is the only way to get ahead in life, that our efforts will lead nowhere because we don't and will never be able to have what it takes to succeed.

On the other hand, having a growth mindset means we believe in the true power of learning. We realize the possibility of expanding our horizons, acquiring new knowledge, and improving our skills. We also know that our intelligence is not static. It can evolve with time and experience.

We're aware of the fact that we can develop any given ability if we have an ardent desire to learn, a resolute determination, and a willingness to put in the effort and work hard. With a growth mindset, we don't shy away from challenges; we embrace them with open arms as we keep pushing through to produce the outcomes we're seeking.

However, no person uses one mindset and one mindset only at all times, and no person is either open to growth or completely closed off. This in itself is a form of fixation and rejection of progression. It's not an either-or type of situation.

You don't live your life with only one particular mindset that governs all of your decisions. While we do have a mindset that is more prevalent than the other, it's not a general rule that applies to everything we do.

We could be open to adjustments and learning moments at work, but we could be reluctant to budge in our relationships with others and vice versa. The goal here is to aim for cultivating a growth mindset in the areas in which we lack that kind of flexibility. We can do that by reframing our thoughts and practicing self-awareness—which leads us to myth #5.

Myth #5: Mental Fitness Is Arbitrary

We all know how important a balanced diet and exercise are for our physical health. We try to cut back on processed foods, we try to squeeze some form of cardio into our packed schedules, we try to cook nutritional meals for ourselves and our families, but when it comes to mental fitness, do we really put in as much effort?

The truth is many people think their minds don't need exercising—besides the mental work it takes to fulfill our professional duties. We assume that mental exertion is a form of mental exercise, so why take it even further? But that weariness is the very opposite of what mental fitness is all about.

Unlike physical activity, exercising our mind muscles is NOT done through overworking and exhausting them. On the contrary, it's allowing them to rest, recover, and break free from the struggles of overthinking. Building self-awareness doesn't have to be strenuous. It's about simply being more mindful of the things we do and how we do them.

If you find your mind too restless for more traditional forms of meditation, you can still make this practice a habit in other ways. Mindfulness is the best 'informal' method to meditate, all while doing other tasks. You don't have to sit in a sensory deprivation tank and free your mind of all thoughts to meditate.

You can do it while making a cup of tea, preparing a meal, taking a walk outside, or doing the most mundane of chores. It's all about bringing your awareness into the activity at hand, paying attention to the present moment, without fear or judgment, but rather with a sense of openness and curiosity.

Research has shown that meditation can help reduce stress and anxiety, boost focus and productivity, improve sleep quality, and enhance emotional regulation. The benefits extend to your physical health as well since meditation is known to lower blood pressure, promote good metabolism, and sustain better breathing.

While you're going about your day, try to stay in the present moment and immerse yourself in what you're doing. If your thoughts lead you somewhere else, acknowledge them, and find your way back to the task at hand. You can use your breath as an anchor, or you can focus on the things around you. Engage all of your senses. What do you see? What do you smell? What do you hear?

Mindfulness is not about freeing your mind from all thoughts and ideas. It's about building awareness of them, seeing them for what they are rather than what you think them to be. So, as you resume your day after reading this, think about the ways in which you can exercise your mind while using mindful meditation.

CHAPTER TWO RECAP:

Our beliefs give us the power to take action and help us create a roadmap to our goals. Limiting beliefs can cause us to miss out on incredible opportunities.

Myth #1 Adversity means regression

Myth #2 Vulnerability is a weakness

Myth #3 I am what I think

Myth #4 If I am not good at it, I never will be—Fixed mindset vs. growth mindset

Myth #5 Mental fitness is arbitrary

PUT IT INTO ACTION

What Are the Facts?

Myth #1 Adversity means regression.

Fact #1 Adversity means growth.

Thought experiment: Think of the most interesting, inspiring person you can—what can you recall about their life or story? Was it easy? Was everything handed to them as they coasted through care-free? Or maybe was there some kind of adversity or possibly a lot of adversity that they had to overcome?

Myth #2 Vulnerability is a weakness.

Fact #2 It takes strength to be vulnerable and seek help.

Thought experiment: Think of the last time someone reached out to you for help or support. What was your reaction? Was it, "Oh gosh, what a weak person, they can't do this for themselves?" or was it "Oh wow, I am so excited to help you. Let's get this together. I'm fully on your team!" Maybe you were even impressed that they were taking that particular endeavour on? Maybe their journey inspired you to be even bolder? Did "weak" even cross your mind?

Myth #3 I am what I think

Fact #3 I am an active agent in my life and "I can"

Thought experiment: There is a way of thinking that involves a through-time perspective that you can harness any time you're feeling consumed by a singular negative thought, emotion, or experience. It's quick and can be developed into a habit with practice! Start by remembering back: that bad test you had in the tenth grade that absolutely meant you were going nowhere in life and were probably going to fail at everything forever . . . did you? In the moment, it may have felt like that bad experience defined you, but through time, that experience faded into a distant memory of little to no consequence. Reframe any current negative experience the same way—more than likely, whatever you're going through will be of little to no consequence at some point in the near future. You are freed from this limiting thought that this moment defines you because it will not.

Myth #4 If I am not good at it, I never will be - Fixed mindset vs. growth mindset.

Fact #4 I am always growing and learning new things.

Thought experiment: Looking to childhood again—remember when you could barely read? Then when you could make out words, but if you had to read out loud, you would have to choose between pronouncing the sounds and understanding what you were saying? I bet that's changed. I bet you've read this entire book so far without thinking about how proficient you are at reading. If not reading, tying your shoes, or adding numbers or anything else that was once challenging but comes easily to you now. Accounting, swimming, design, public speaking . . . embodying the attitude of a first grader learning how to read, you can tackle anything and become an expert in time! You are always growing and learning new things!

Myth #5 Mental fitness is arbitrary

Fact #5 Mental fitness, like physical fitness, can drastically enhance your quality of life!

Thought experiment: Neuroplasticity refers to the physical structure of the human brain and can change with thoughts and behaviours—including meditation! Behavioural and thought patterns form neural pathways that can change the physical structure and connections in your brain. The stronger the neural pathway, the easier that thought or behaviour becomes. Thought patterns of self-love, for example, can strengthen your ability to think positively about yourself. Write an affirmation (positive statement) about yourself and repeat it as often as you can to yourself for a week (try at least once a day). It may feel strange at first, but by day 7, notice how it feels easier to believe yourself. You've just strengthened the neural pathways of self-love and changed your brain!

Notes

We change our behavior when the pain of staying the same becomes greater than the pain of changing. Consequences give us the pain that motivates us to change.

- Dr. Henry Cloud & Dr. John Townsend

If you spend your life sparing people's feelings and feeding their vanity, you get so you can't distinguish what should be respected in them.

- F. Scott Fitzgerald

When we fail to set boundaries and hold people accountable, we feel used and mistreated. This is why we sometimes attack who they are, which is far more hurtful than addressing a behavior or a choice.

- Brené Brown

SUCCESS BEGINS WITH A WINNING MINDSET

We've come to fall in love with the idea of success, or at least how the concept of success is presented to us by society. There are people who live their lives believing that the success they aim to achieve is simply unattainable, while others look up to successful people in their industries and take strides to absorb every bit of knowledge they share.

Reaching a level of success that your inner critic will be proud of almost seems impossible, and most people will go about accomplishing this lifelong goal the wrong way. Walking in the footsteps of the individuals that inspire you is not a bad start, but a blind pursuit can often divert your focus from the things that matter to you. No one path is the same, and you can't know where somebody started or what will delineate their finish line. Finding success begins with identifying your purpose and what drives you. This cannot happen without evaluating your dominant mindset in the three fundamental aspects of your life: wealth, health, and relationships.

Your Success Hinges on Your Mindset

We live in an abundant time in human history, one filled with promise and change. Change comes from all different angles, pushing us to adapt, learn, test, and challenge ourselves on a daily basis.

If we stay focused on our inflexibility, if we keep telling ourselves, "I don't deal well with the unexpected" or "I can't cope with change," those beliefs will condition not just the way we approach money and wealth, but our health and relationships as well.

Letting go of your fixed mindset and adopting a growth mindset has the power to change your worldview and attract exciting opportunities your way. In this section, we will start by exploring how the right growth mindset can influence the level of success you can achieve, be it financially, professionally, or personally.

How a Growth Mindset Can Lead to Financial Success

Money: a source of happiness or the root of all evil?

Money is such a loaded topic, perhaps even verging on the taboo. Some people feel awkward or embarrassed to talk about it when it's brought up in conversation, while others completely avoid the subject and deflect the discussion in another direction.

Maybe the reason it's out of bounds in social contexts is the many notions and issues we associate with it. We often hear phrases like "money isn't everything," "money can't buy happiness," or "money shouldn't be your only goal in life."

We're told we're too blunt if we bring it up, and we're told we're too materialistic when most of our concerns are centered around money. At the same time, if we don't express an ardent interest in wealth, and if we don't communicate our passion for it, we're criticized for our idealism and naiveté.

We're told that we're gullible, that we don't know how the world works, and that real life is not a utopia. Either way, it seems like we're forced to join one side or the other. There are all kinds of assumptions about money and financial wealth, villainizing the people who have it and resenting the people who pursue it.

There is a fictional belief that every rich person is inherently manipulating, conniving, and contriving dreadful schemes, that wealth is somehow wrong, and the people who attain it should be condemned for all the evils and injustices of the world.

But if we strip it from all these negative and positive connotations, if we take it as what it is rather than what everyone thinks it is or thinks it should be, money is very simple to define. It's a tool of exchange like all others.

"What's in your head determines what's in your wallet."

"Never spend your money before you have earned it"

—Thomas Jefferson

Money can buy you comfort and peace of mind. It can allow you to produce valuable goods and services. It can make your life easier, but it can also help you make other people's lives easier as well. You can invest it in doing good and making a difference in the world.

You can use it to bring happiness to the people you love and care about. Money is and can be the root of good if you allow it to be. It's all about the way you perceive it and your intentions of using it. It's what you use to cover medical expenses, luxuriate in hotels, and pay for vacations.

Money is also what allows you to have food on the table and a roof over your head. But a big part of attracting the right opportunities is all about the mindset you have. If you build all these negative associations with money, this will be reflected in the thoughts you have and the beliefs you hold about yourself. Your attitude will end up pushing money away from you. So, you can either get on the road to financial freedom and turn this year from one of unprecedented crisis to one of unprecedented wealth, or you can let your mental state determine your financial fate!

How a Growth Mindset Can Lead to Personal Success

When you build self-awareness around the thoughts you have and the self-talk you engage in, you begin to harness the power of creating your own reality. By redirecting your negativity towards more constructive and positive energy, every atom in your body starts to react accordingly.

This is the law of attraction in its essence. Like attracts like. So, when you take active steps towards a healthier and more fulfilling life, you also begin to attract like-minded people. Opening yourself up to the world of possibilities out there allows you to build and nurture strong bonds with others.

As a result, your relationships will begin to improve. Moreover, surrounding yourself with positive people who have a growth mind-set gives you the opportunity to learn and evolve. It also eliminates unnecessary external stressors as you find that you have an expansive support system of creative and innovative people to fall back on.

This, in turn, affects your attitude, your perception of the world, and by extension, your behaviour. When you're in a good mental state, you also tend to focus more on your body's needs, including physical health. You're more prone to cultivate better habits and let go of toxic and destructive ones.

How to switch your mindset and attract opportunities your way

You can develop your own growth mindset worksheet to track your progress and touch base with every aspect of your life. Here are three actions you can take now that will fully transform your life to be more abundant, positive, and full of exciting possibilities.

View your peers through the lens of teamwork and learning opportunities: Instead of viewing someone who is better than you as a threat, think of all the things you can learn from them and the doors they could open for you. The people you think are intimidating or threatening may have the expertise and insight you're looking for to get unstuck. They may help you obtain answers to a problem that you've never thought of or considered before. Shift your thinking and recognize that every person you encounter is an opportunity for you to see things from a different angle. The fact that they're more experienced isn't something to shy away from; it's rather one to embrace!

Stay true to your values: They are your internal compass, and they are what will help you stay grounded in the face of adversity. When you're more assertive about your principles, you're guiding the people around you to respect your boundaries. Moreover, when the goals you set for yourself align with what matters the most to you, the outcome will be much more rewarding. As a result, you will be in a much better mental state, and your health will thrive. Engaging in pursuits and ventures that regularly connect to your intrinsic values instead of extrinsic ones can lead you to an abundance of successes in all three aspects of your life; wealth, health, and relationships.

Keep your "why" close: One of the most fundamental steps of setting goals and attracting the right opportunities is your "why". This is what drives you to seek financial wealth and independence, what propels you to build strong relationships, and what pushes you to improve your mental and physical health. Your why is essential because it helps you see the bigger picture and find inner motivation despite how challenging or difficult a time you're going through.

The right growth mindset will only attract opportunities your way if you're fully aware of how your perception shapes your reality. You have the power to draw more successes your way. Know that whatever you put out into the world, the same energy will come back to you.

Not every opportunity is the "right" one!

Dreaming is an inherent part of charting out your aspirations and figuring out what you want from life. And when you're more open and welcoming, the universe will reward you. With that said, not every dream is worth pursuing, and not every opportunity is the right one.

Finding your purpose in life means you have to be more selective about the things you love and accept that you can't entertain every thought that pops up in your mind. Focusing on the bigger picture when temptations emerge is essential. Setting boundaries and recognizing the opportunities that further your "why" will be a major part of your success timeline.

The Hedgehog Concept

The Hedgehog Concept is based on an ancient Greek parable that poet Archilochus wrote. He said, "The fox knows many things, but the hedgehog knows one big thing." In the parable, the fox knows many strategies and uses different tactics to try and catch the hedgehog. Yet, every time, the fox is defeated. It fails to recognize that the hedgehog knows how to do one major thing perfectly, and that is defending itself.

Often, when asked to choose between being a fox or being a hedgehog, most people will opt for the former rather than the latter. Perhaps because they value how fast, sleek, and cunning a fox is, compared to the slow, prickly, and plodding hedgehog. After all, a fox's knowledge and interests are broader than a hedgehog's.

But the hedgehog's entire purpose resides in the simplicity of what it does. A simplicity that helps create one clear yet powerful point of focus. If you're constantly pursuing different ventures, starting new projects, abandoning half-finished ones, and taking on more than you can handle, not only will your attention be scattered, but you also won't excel in any of those particular interests.

Multitasking is no longer a highly prized skill. On the contrary, it's all about knowing what you're good at and seeking to become great at it, to excel in that one domain rather than to try your hand at this thing then the next.

Based on this parable, there are two types of people: foxes and hedgehogs. Foxes have a tendency to jump from one strategy to the next. Their cognitive style is more nuanced; they try different solutions and are comfortable with contradictions. On the other hand, hedgehogs focus on the big picture. They have a cunning ability to reduce every occurring issue to one organizing principle; they're more decisive and are hence considered better equipped for leadership roles.

Finding your life's purpose starts by identifying the one thing you do best. If you keep chasing many goals at the same time, you will achieve very little. But if you channel your energy and focus into one cohesive and unified goal, only then will you know true success.

Three strategies to live your purpose with a growth mindset

Both the hedgehog's concept and the Japanese concept of Ikigai (loosely translated as purpose in life or reason to live) explain that living your purpose is that ideal point of intersection between what you love, what the world needs, what you excel at, and what you can be paid for.

Adopting a growth mindset can help you cultivate your passion and turn it into something you can get paid for.

Set clear goals and take action

Reflect on what you're passionate about at work, what makes you excited to get up in the morning, and what drives you to persevere. Then think about what you can do better than anyone else you know, that one thing that is utterly and entirely yours. This is your purpose in life. But knowing your Ikigai or hedgehog's concept is not enough.

If you want success, you need to work for it. You need to set up a plan and take action. You have to start by setting clear goals for what you want to achieve. With that said, simply being aware of where you want to end up is not sufficient on its own.

You also have to craft an action plan that will get you there. This is what will help you stay on track throughout your journey. That, and having a coach to guide you, inspire you, and help you develop a growth mindset. And that is where I come in!

When you have a growth mindset, you look forward to challenges, despite how intimidating they may be. Moreover, you're prepared to work for your goals, no matter how much time and effort it takes to accomplish them.

Focus on effort and practice for continuous improvement

"Good is the enemy of great. [...] Few people attain great lives, in large part because it is just so easy to settle for a good life."

- Jim Collins

Living your true purpose means finding that one big thing you can do better than everybody else. That doesn't mean you have to be the best at it already, but for you to be a hedgehog, you need to invest in continuous improvement to eventually excel at that one thing. Naturally, this won't happen overnight. You need to be intentional, let your enthusiasm fuel your motivation, and continuously focus on your personal growth, learning, and development. Remember, never settle for half-hearted efforts!

Conquer your fears and persist through failure

Fear is the number one thing that holds us back from unlocking our potential and living our purpose. Sometimes, the crippling anticipation of failure prevents us from even trying in the first place. This is all due to having a fixed mindset, where we think that our abilities and skills must be innate, thus, unchangeable.

On the other hand, when we move into a growth mindset, we come to learn that through practice and perseverance, we can develop those skills and abilities. We also understand that true learning and self-improvement cannot happen without making mistakes or failing.

In fact, mistakes and failures are inevitable, but it's important that when we do fail, we also remember to get right back up. This isn't just about resilience, it's also about learning from those mistakes and persisting to do and to become better.

Living your purpose doesn't have to be an unattainable dream. It's not too good to be true either. By identifying that perfect intersection between what your passion is, what you're great at, what the world needs, and what you can be paid for, you can then work on developing tangible goals to get you from where you currently are to where you want to be. And having a growth mindset will definitely help speed that process!

CHAPTER THREE RECAP:

Finding success begins with identifying your purpose and what drives you.

Your success hinges on your mindset, so focus on letting go of your fixed mindset and adopting a growth mindset. It will influence your levels of success financially, personally, and professionally.

Mindset shifts:

Financial: Money mindset—money is a tool of exchange like all others.

Personal: Wellness mindset—when you take steps towards your own wellness, you attract others with similar mindsets that, in turn, cultivate healthy relationships and feedback into your wellness journey.

Professional: Success mindset—your peers are your learning tools and teammates, your values are your compass, and your "why" is your direction—wield these tools!

The Hedgehog Concept—The fox knows many things, but the hedgehog knows one big thing. The simplicity of the hedgehog helps create one clear, powerful point of focus that is highly conducive to success.

Strategies to live your purpose with a growth mindset:

One: Set clear goals and take action

Two: Focus on effort and practice for continuous improvement

Three: Conquer your fears and persist through failure

Notes

Resilience is accepting your new reality, even if it's less good than the one you had before. You can fight it, you can do nothing but scream about what you've lost, or you can accept that and try to put together something that's good.

- Elizabeth Edwards

The human capacity for burden is like bamboo—far more flexible than you'd ever believe at first glance.

- Jodi Picoult

I can be changed by what happens to me. But I refuse to be reduced by it.

- Maya Angelou

REALIZING EMOTIONAL RESILIENCE

Story time. In my life, I've had my emotional resilience tested on numerous occasions, like many people. For some of us, there is a defining challenge that we can identify that changed us in a larger way and allows us to reflect on our own growth. This is one of those.

Finding great mentors in life is an extraordinary thing. I had a mentor who meant a great deal to me and inspired me in my own ambitions and life choices. The relationship broke down through a series of events. I was left to really explore my values and how far I was willing to go to defend them. Being challenged to stand my ground forced me to become my own advocate in a situation that blindsided me. I was presented with the involuntary opportunity to redefine the trajectory I thought I was on. It was a big moment, and being disappointed by someone you look up to is a specific kind of emotional blow. My resilience was undeniably tested. Facing a dramatic shift in perspective throughout this period of time, the challenge of questioning my self-worth, the importance of reflecting upon and controlling my emotions, and persevering through when I didn't know what the result would be, allowed me to come out of the experience with stronger bonds not only with myself but with the people and beliefs that made my resilience possible. The roller coaster of emotions wasn't always pretty, but in the end, being able to harness that experience for the betterment of my own life and the lives of others is empowering beyond words.

At one point or the other, we've all had our emotional resilience tested. Sometimes, it's not as horrible an experience, and we are able to collect ourselves, calm our frantic minds, stand up, and rise to the challenge.

Other times, it's too overwhelming, and we feel like we will never be the same person again, that our lives will never have that comforting sense of normalcy, that whatever it is we're dealing with will never get resolved.

If we let it, what feels like a bad day can easily turn into two, then three, then a week, then a month . . . every day we wake up, a tiny sliver of hope fills our hearts: Maybe today will be different, maybe today I will be myself again. Then it isn't, and you aren't either.

So, you beat yourself up because you couldn't be "strong," and you couldn't get past your feelings and emotions. But that is NOT what emotional resilience is! You don't have to suppress your emotions to be strong.

You don't have to put on a facade every time you step out the door. Find strength in your emotions and feelings, but also engage your mind to identify where they come from. That's how you deal with adversity, and that's how you overcome hardships.

Emotional resilience isn't a standard. It's not a fixed way to manage problems, it's subjective, and it varies from one person to the next. What empowers you isn't necessarily the same element that inspires and motivates those around you.

Realizing emotional resilience involves many things, and repressing your fears and worries isn't one of them. This chapter delves into the five pillars of emotional resilience (flexibility, self-esteem, emotional control, persistence, and strong relationships) and how these can help you cultivate and maintain a sense of stability in the face of difficulties.

Pillar #1: Flexibility

Flexibility is often conflated with self-denial. Being flexible doesn't mean being accommodating to everyone else's wants and needs while sacrificing your own. It doesn't mean always being the one to adjust, adapt, and compromise, nor does it mean to tiptoe your way around that of others.

You can be flexible and still maintain your principles and values. You can be adaptable and still allow others the space to express themselves. Flexibility should never be a coping mechanism for guilt, shame, or embarrassment. It should stem from an innate desire to rise above daily challenges and solve problems in a way that is true to who you are and what you stand for.

Being flexible is having the ability to effectively assess a situation to consider both optimistic and pessimistic outcomes. So, you're able to examine the positives and the negatives before making a judgment or a decision.

When it comes to building emotional resilience, you have to fluidly shift from a positive to a negative perspective. Otherwise, you won't be able to see the bigger picture or gauge the magnitude of a given situation.

We're always being told to view life from a positive standpoint; that negativity and pessimism will only set us back. But pessimism is important sometimes. Now before you gasp or scream, "Preposterous!" —there's actual science behind it.

This concept is called inversion. Merriam-Webster defines inversion as "a reversal of position, order, form, or relationship." For instance, inversion is when you put the verb before its subject. Similarly, adopting an inversion mindset means you start with the outcome you don't want to achieve to get to the outcome you're seeking.

If a fear cannot be articulated, it can't be conquered.

- Stephen King

In this way, if you're facing a challenge, you reflect on all those "worst-case scenarios" you're always running away from. This can be incredibly insightful in identifying fears that are often too vague or unnamed, but it's also helpful to explore those unwanted outcomes. When you do so, you can carefully craft an action plan to achieve what you want all while having a safety net to fall back on in case things derail.

Pillar #2: Self-esteem

This is one of the most important pillars of emotional resilience. Self-esteem can be defined in many ways, it includes self-awareness, self-acceptance, self-confidence, but it also goes way beyond those personality constructs.

Self-esteem is our perception of ourselves, our perception of our worth and value, but also the level of respect we show ourselves and how well we can maintain our boundaries. This is a vital component of emotional resilience because it encompasses all these micro components that are absolutely necessary for us to build and nurture a healthy concept of the world and our place in it.

But because this is such a broad and expansive ideal, it also brings with it a lot of confusion and misconceptions. Some mistake having healthy self-esteem for exuding a confident facade, while others associate self-esteem with a ruthless ability to blatantly reject (or perhaps even hurt) others without feeling guilty. This couldn't be further from the truth.

We've all struggled with self-esteem issues at one point or the other, whether it's our self-image and how insecure we feel about it or whether it's allowing ourselves to be doormats for others to walk over. We shouldn't feel embarrassed to admit it, and we shouldn't feel fearful either.

The truth is self-esteem is something we develop from our early childhood and on. The environment we grew up in, the people we were around, and the circumstances we found ourselves in all contribute to our perceptions of ourselves (physically, mentally, and emotionally).

And while we cannot change our past, our parents, and our siblings, we can change how we let their thoughts, feelings, and behaviour affect us. We have control over the present, and we have influence over the here and now. Self-acceptance starts with accepting ourselves despite the mistakes we've made or the things we did wrong. It should be mindful, free of judgment, full of empathy and compassion.

If we cannot come to terms with the past, we will never be able to live in the present and embrace the promises of the future. After acceptance of the things we cannot change comes the courage to change the things we can, the things that are within our control.

This includes building our confidence, establishing healthy boundaries with ourselves and others, learning to assert our wants and needs, as well as starting to live and speak our truth. Only then will we be able to become more comfortable with who we are.

Tips for building self-confidence

Keep a brag book. Instead of being focused on all the things you did wrong, all the mistakes you made, and all the failures you accumulated, focus on your achievements, on all that you managed to accomplish, and all the successes you've compiled. Then document all of those successes in a brag book. Whenever you find yourself mentally regressing into a negative headspace, go over your brag book to remind yourself of your top hits.

Visualize yourself as you want to be. "What the mind can conceive and believe it can achieve." —Napoleon Hill. Visualization is a powerful tool that allows you to see the best version of yourself in your own mind. When we have low self-confidence, we also tend to struggle with a poor perception of ourselves. Practicing visualization can help you get out of that rut and see yourself basking in the successes you can achieve.

Practice positive affirmations

Attitude is a choice. Happiness is a choice. Optimism is a choice. Kindness is a choice. Giving is a choice. Respect is a choice. Whatever choice you make makes you. Choose wisely.

- Roy T. Bennett

Because we tend to behave in accordance with the image we have of ourselves, changing how we view ourselves through the power of positive affirmations can help us make a lasting change in our self-confidence.

Challenge your inner critic

Give space to your thoughts, clear the noise in your head, chit-chat with your inner critic, decide and move on.

- Cristina Imre

Some of the harshest criticism that we get comes from ourselves. Questioning your inner critic and challenging it can take away its power. Instead, seek your own approval and find opportunities to reward yourself even for the smallest of wins.

Create personal boundaries

If you live your life to please everyone else, you will continue to feel frustrated and powerless. This is because what others want may not be good for you. You are not being mean when you say NO to unreasonable demands or when you express your ideas, feelings, and opinions, even if they differ from those of others.

—Beverly Engel

Learn to say "no" and to ask for what you want, teach the people around you to respect your boundaries, because the more say you have over your life, the greater your self-confidence will be.

Redirect yourself towards an equality mentality

If you give yourself a chance to get to know your positive inner-self better, you would never have a need to be someone else.

—Edmond Mbiaka.

Often, when we're struggling with our confidence, we tend to view others as better or more deserving than we are. Instead of allowing this belief to dictate our lives, we need to start seeing ourselves as equals to everybody else. This is key to developing a healthier image of who we are and where we stand.

Pillar #3: Emotional control

We often mistake emotional control for suppressing our feelings and emotions. We assume that we have to be objective, rational, and analytical to be a great leader. While those are essential qualities to have, a great leader should also connect with team members, empathize, listen, and make sure they feel seen and heard.

A big part of leadership is motivating your team and encouraging their self-expression. True leadership allows your team members to be comfortable in who they are all while working towards a common goal.

It's also inspiring them to adopt those goals as their own. Emotional control is not repressing your emotions or stepping over the feelings of others, it's being able to recognize that sadness, frustration, stress, and anger, so you can channel that intensity into accomplishing what you're setting out to do.

Self-control is denying yourself those quick fixes and the temporary relief they bring with them because you know better than to succumb to temptation and, most importantly, because you're aware of how rewarding the bigger goal would be.

Emotional control is acknowledging your feelings but also examining where they come from and why before jumping to conclusions. It's thinking before taking the leap, but it's also being considerate of how that leap affects you and others around you.

When you're more mindful of your emotions, whether they stem from a place of fear or a place of despair, you're less likely to be overwhelmed, especially when things don't go as planned. You trust yourself and your team members to rise above the challenge no matter how difficult it seems.

Pillar #4: Persistence

Persistence is the foundation of emotional resilience. It's what pushes you to persevere despite external stressors. It's what keeps your inner motivation alive and what drives you to do your best and accomplish your goals. Persistence also allows you to develop the consistency and commitment you need to keep moving forward.

Whether you're dealing with a setback or internal conflict, your determination to learn and grow will help you power through difficulties. Your persistence doesn't need to be blindly optimistic. On the contrary, it gives you a chance to be positive but also realistic about the way the world works.

No need to put on the delusional rose-coloured glasses. No need to put on dark cloudy lenses either. Unlike blind optimism or blatant pessimism, being persistent means you can examine a situation with its pros and cons. You pay attention to both the negative and positive information that is relevant to the problems you face.

You know a lost cause when you see one, you recognize when to disengage in the face of insolvencies, but you also trust your gut to know when to keep going and press on. Knowing when to cut your losses is an essential quality that very few people have. It's equally as important as knowing when to stay the course and carry on. A key element to building emotional resilience is sticking to your goals and resolutions, even if, or especially when that pushes you to face your fears.

Pillar #5: Strong relationships

Having strong interpersonal relationships is both a by-product and a prerequisite of emotional resilience. If you have the power to build and maintain healthy personal bonds with others, both at work and outside of work, then you have already taken the first step towards a resilient life.

We are social creatures by nature, even the most introverted of us, and being around others gives us the strength to endure difficult times, overcome our problems, and evolve from them. The experience of cultivating and nurturing strong relationships changes you at the deepest of levels. It shapes the way you see the world and how you view yourself.

So, to build emotional resilience, we first need to develop our capacity to improve our interpersonal relationships and open ourselves to build new ones. As a result, our emotional intelligence sharpens, and so do our coping mechanisms.

Although we tend to think of ourselves as open-minded and non-judgmental, sometimes, we don't give other people the chance they deserve, whether it be out of fear or self-preservation, we're quick to put them in a box, slap a label on it, and move on. While first impressions are important, they're not everything.

Making a hasty conclusion about someone or building a set of assumptions based on one or two things they said isn't fair to that person, but it's also not fair to yourself. We've all had the tendency to categorize and compartmentalize, perhaps because we don't like the unknown, and we're not very fond of how unstable or unpredictable it might be.

Despite your disinclination to the unexpected, if you take a step forward with a more open mindset, you may be surprised at the qualities other people have. No matter how different they are from you, there's always something to learn, and there's always an opportunity for growth and personal development, though only if you allow it to manifest!

Making sure to cultivate and nurture these five pillars is essential to developing and realizing your emotional resilience. However, this can only happen when the things you do on a daily basis are in alignment with the values you hold dearest.

Practicing Your Values is the Key to Emotional Resilience

Your values not only dictate the way you live but the beliefs you're not willing to compromise on and the causes you are prepared to fight for. When you practice your values, this means that your thoughts, feelings, words, and behaviour all correlate with those beliefs.

What Happens When You're Not Living in Alignment with Your Values?

When you're not living in alignment with your values, you're spending the majority of your time and energy doing things that aren't meaningful or important to you. This could be working overtime all throughout the week while what you value the most is spending quality time with your family.

Or going to a monotonous and systematic desk job when what you value the most are art and creativity. Or even being a stay-at-home parent when all you can think about is the career you had to sacrifice.

Living out of alignment with your values can manifest as many things, but most notably; resentment, anger, and frustration. This discord and deep dissatisfaction with what you're doing gradually build up into this monstrous feeling of unfulfillment.

So, you start to blame the people around you for the sacrifices and compromises you had to make, even if they played no part at all in the decisions you took. The longer you live this way, the more out of sync with your core self you become.

You begrudgingly get out of bed every morning, dreading the thought of forcing yourself to do things that have very little meaning to you all over again. You're constantly stressed, anxious, angry, and bitter.

Being in misalignment with your values not only makes you unhappy but also makes you closed, rigid, and resistant. This is the opposite of the flexibility, adaptability, and openness that come with emotional resilience.

So, you feel like there's no way out of this cycle, that if you were to be more true to your values, you'd have to uproot your life and drastically change who you are. This couldn't be further from the truth. You can live a life in true alignment with what you value, and become more emotionally resilient, all without the pain of feeling miserable and inadequate.

Stay True to Your Values to Build Emotional Resilience

You may be thinking, "Just because I believe in being open to opportunities around me, the importance of living new experiences and exploring the world, doesn't mean I can afford to quit my job and follow my passion in life," or "I value my career and I know I am capable of great things if I were to focus all my time and energy on my job, but my partner won't be pleased if I don't stay home full-time to take care of our children."

These are completely understandable concerns. In some cases, you will need to adjust your responsibilities and duties with your core values and passions. Living truthfully and authentically won't come easily. There will be compromises to make, you may have to break some rules, deal with judgment from others, and even upset some people.

At the end of the day, knowing that your values are what brings meaning to your life and what makes everything worthwhile, you can avoid any feelings of guilt or shame. When you dare to be brave enough and start living in alignment with your values, you will also find the inner strength and resilience needed to face all the negativity and overcome your fears.

When you take that first step off the path of extrinsic values and direct yourself towards intrinsic ones, you become more in sync with the true nature of your mind, body, and spirit. Even if the work is exhausting, time-consuming, and difficult at times, you will still feel fulfilled and satisfied because you're doing what truly matters to you.

And because you're catering more to your wants and needs as

well as your well-being and happiness, you gradually start to build your emotional resilience. Ultimately, you won't feel as stressed because you managed to create an environment and nurture relationships that support your aspirations, encourage your growth and development, and also help you navigate change and adversity more smoothly.

PUT IT INTO ACTION:

Three practical Steps to Align Your Values for Greater Emotional Resilience

Step #1: Get your notepad and write down a brief account of all the significant moments you've had that taught you something important about your life. You may have quite a long list, so work on grouping them into different categories, especially if you can summarize that lesson into one word.

Step #2: Now highlight the moments that represent who you truly are, and in a different colour, those that represent who you want to grow into. Next, select five core values that are deeply meaningful to you and that you are intentional with.

Step #3: Review your actions and decisions and whether those align with your core values at the end of each day. Ask yourself the following questions.

Which values come more naturally to me?

Which values feel inauthentic or out of alignment?

Which values are difficult to live by? Why?

Are there any values I need to reconsider, add, or adjust?

Living our core values is integral to living a life with purpose and meaning. There is no greater gift we can offer ourselves than that of honouring our authenticity, who we truly are, and living with passion.

When our personal values align with our thoughts, feelings, and behaviour, we experience more joy, happiness, fulfillment, and contentment. We're proud of our life's legacy, and we're better equipped to deal with adversity, difficulties, as well as challenging situations.

CHAPTER FOUR RECAP:

Emotional resilience is tested throughout our lives, and there is no fixed way to measure it. There are pillars that we can focus our energy on in order to realize our own emotional resilience and strengthen it.

Pillar #1: Flexibility: the fluidity to shift perspective

Pillar #2: Self-esteem: self-awareness, self-acceptance, and self-confidence

Tips for being self-confident:

Keep a brag book

Visualize yourself as you want to be

Practice positive affirmations

Challenge your inner critic

Create personal boundaries

Redirect yourself toward an equality mentality

Pillar #3: Emotional control: —acknowledging feelings, examining where they came from, and focusing on a long-term solution rather than a quick-fix

Pillar #4: Persistence: —foundation of emotional resilience pushing you to persevere despite external stressors

Pillar #5: Strong relationships: —a by-product and prerequisite of emotional resilience

---

Go to **www.amanda-dasilva.com/visualizations** for more!

Notes

Change might not be fast, and it isn't always easy. But with time and effort, almost any habit can be reshaped.

- Charles Duhigg

We become what we repeatedly do.

- Sean Covey

You'll never change your life until you change something you do daily. The secret of your success is found in your daily routine.

- John C. Maxwell

BUILDING A BETTER YOU: HABITS FOR SUCCESS

We all know what it takes to stay physically fit, a good exercise regimen, a healthy balanced diet, and a strong will to keep going despite temptation. Staying mentally fit requires training your brain with exercises to boost your memory, creativity, and thinking skills. But we often forget about our emotional fitness.

We cater to the body's needs, to the mind's needs, yet when it comes to our emotions, we don't know where to begin. Trying to succeed as a leader within your own life, you probably have encountered your fair share of heart-wrenching moments, moments that tested your faith, your endurance, and your patience, sometimes all three simultaneously.

We tend to think of success as something we have or seek to obtain. We believe once we acquire this prized possession, it belongs to us, and we own it. But success is not something you have, it's something you do, or choose to do, over and over again.

To be successful, you have to be prepared to endure the hardships and setbacks which are an inherent part of any life journey. You need to make sure that no trial you come across is wasted. Allow each challenge to tend to your personal growth and development, to boost your patience, your faith, your fortitude, as well as your humility.

Every hardship you go through, combined with your ability to stay determined and persevere, builds your character, purifies your mindset, and catapults you toward success. Much like other types of fitness, how great of a leader and person you become is a direct result of what hardships you are willing to undergo.

But no matter how determined you are, this cannot happen if you're not also disciplined. Discipline is the byproduct and the end result of having a set daily routine that caters to all important aspects of your life: physical, mental, and emotional fitness.

When you allocate some part of your day to cater to each element, you will feel fulfilled and more in control. You will also be prepared to face any obstacles head-on because you trust your ability to maintain calm amidst the storm.

Building better habits is key to cultivating and maintaining discipline. In this chapter, we discuss the six essential steps to develop healthier habits for bigger successes.

Six steps to developing the habits of success

According to experts, forming a new habit can take anywhere from 18 days to 254 days. This depends on how drastic of a change this habit is from what you're used to. On average, you will need 66 days for your new habit to become natural and automatic and 21 days to form a habit of medium complexity.

This concerns simpler habits like getting up earlier, meditating each morning, doing some form of exercise, going to bed at a set hour, planning every day in advance, beginning your day with the most important or most challenging task, completing one task at a time, etc.

You can develop these habits in three weeks, and the more you practice, the less you're likely to slack off. The goal is to develop better habits that are so ingrained in your daily routine that you would feel something's amiss if you don't do them.

But how do you develop these habits and stick to them even when you're feeling uninspired and unmotivated? There's a simple methodology that is a guaranteed recipe for success, six essential steps to help you acquire any habit you desire.

Step #1: Be decisive about your resolutions

When it comes to resolutions, determination is key. You need to be clearly decisive about the routine you want to establish. If you aim to rise earlier and meditate first thing in the morning, set an alarm for that specific time, and as soon as it goes off, get out of bed immediately, go to your designated meditation space and begin your session. Don't allow your brain room for hesitation or doubt.

The minute you start questioning your decision, you've already lost the battle. Your mind will probably do everything it can to convince you that 20 more minutes of sleep is detrimental to your survival, and we all know how hard winning those debates is. Shut out your inner monologue and believe in the decisions you made.

Step #2: Never allow exceptions

During the formative stages of your new habit pattern, your resolutions need to remain unflinching. You can't allow yourself to make any exceptions, especially in the beginning. No excuses or rationalizations either because those will only lead you to question your decisions and act in discordance with what you want your routine to be.

If you want to wake up at 6:30 a.m., then you need to discipline yourself to get up at 6:30 a.m. every single day until it becomes automatic. If you want to get 45 minutes of exercise, then you need to squeeze that into your daily routine no matter what happens, no matter how much you're dreading it.

Step #3: Inform those around you

Sometimes, it's harder to stick to new habits when the people around you influence a major part of your day. You want to be nice and accommodating, but you also want to stick to your resolutions and succeed at establishing a new habit pattern.

If you're on a diet or you're trying to eat healthier, it can be hard to refuse the heavenly desserts your partner always makes or those scrumptious cookies your colleague brought to work—you don't want to be rude after all.

But if you want to succeed at breaking the cycle, you need to inform those around you of your resolutions and decisions. In addition to asserting your decisions, this will also keep you accountable when you're aware others are watching you to see if you will follow through with your resolutions.

Step #4: Visualize where you want to be

Visualization is a powerful technique when it comes to setting new habits. When you see yourself performing the behaviour you're aiming for, your mind assimilates that image and works on translating this new reality into your life.

So, the more often you visualize yourself acting according to your new habits, the more rapidly your subconscious mind will accept this pattern of behaviour.

Visualization also provides you with a portrayal of all the rewarding emotions and feelings associated with following through with these resolutions. And because your mind wants those good feelings to substantialize, it will work harder to make them come true.

Step #5: Create affirmations that reinforce your objectives

Positive affirmations can act as a powerful trigger to internalize the behaviour you want to implement into your daily routine. When you repeat the affirmations over and over again, especially out loud, this repetition dramatically increases the speed at which you're prone to develop these new habits.

For example, you can start with something like, "Each morning, I wake up at 6:30 a.m. and get going." Try to repeat those words throughout the day but especially right before you go to bed. You'll find that most mornings, you will wake up minutes before your alarm goes off, and soon enough, you won't even need to set an alarm at all. You can do the same for your entire habit-building resolution.

PUT IT INTO ACTION:

Habit affirmations: Write the following affirmations on sticky notes and keep them in sight (near your desk, on your fridge, on your bathroom mirror, etc.) The more you repeat them, the easier it will become to let go of old unwanted habits and make room for healthy new ones.

Every day I am developing new and positive habits.

Each time I challenge a past habit, I feel a greater sense of control and self-esteem.

Day by day, I am gaining more control over my past habits.

Changing my behaviour is as easy as changing my thoughts.

All my habits support me in positive ways.

All my habits are positive and beneficial.

All habits in my life are health-giving.

Step # 6: Reward yourself consistently

In addition to the satisfaction you get from following through with your resolutions, you also need to reward yourself for reaffirming and reinforcing new habits. When you do this, your subconscious mind will begin to associate the pleasure of the reward with that particular behaviour.

In this way, you're creating a new reality of positive consequences that you subconsciously look forward to as a result of sticking to your new routine. Besides conditioning your mind to anticipate compensation for its efforts, you also deserve to celebrate your wins, no matter how small they are!

 # Bonus Tip: Be persistent and take accountability

Practice makes perfect, so resolve to persist. Building a better you is a journey like any other. It takes patience, perseverance, and strong determination. Moving toward self-improvement and personal development can be arduous.

It often requires a lot of time and effort, but the destination you're headed to will be most rewarding. So be accountable for your behaviour, channel motivation from within, and trust the process.

CHAPTER FIVE RECAP:

Staying mentally fit requires training your brain with exercises to boost your memory, creativity, and thinking skills. But we often forget about our emotional fitness.

Six steps to developing the habits of success:

Step 1: Be decisive about your resolutions.

Step 2: Never allow exceptions.

Step 3: Inform those around you.

Step 4: Visualize where you want to be.

Step 5: Create affirmations that reinforce your objectives.

Step 6: Reward yourself consistently.

Bonus tip: Be persistent and take accountability.

Notes

Don't be pushed around by the fears in your mind. Be led by the dreams in your heart.

- Roy T. Bennett

It's not the load that breaks you down, it's the way you carry it.

- Lou Holtz

When we are no longer able to change a situation, we are challenged to change ourselves.

- Viktor E. Frankl

DAILY ROUTINES TO STAY MOTIVATED

Changing your life is a slow process. There is no switch you can flip and have everything magically fall into place. You must be willing to persevere through the hard times, and no matter how challenging or difficult life gets, your ability to push through those walls and run those obstacles over will set you apart and set you up for success.

The truth is you don't need to make big changes all at once to see big results. In fact, little tweaks in your daily routine can go a long way when it comes to building better habits and becoming more productive.

With the right set of practices and the perfect amount of emotional resilience, you will accomplish all of your goals in good time. The best way to start is by making those small changes and taking this journey one step at a time.

Three Daily Routines for Building a Better You

There are a few habits you can incorporate into your day that will make a significant impact on your productivity and development as a person. These are three daily routines that will transform your life.

Mindfulness practices & daily meditation strategies

Our monotonous lifestyle is slowly making us more automated in the way we live our lives. Sometimes we're so consumed by the stress of the "daily grind" that we can't notice things around us. From the way we commute, to the way we work, watch TV, eat, and communicate.

This is why being more mindful of the way you live your life is so revolutionary, especially in these difficult times.

Our work life can be automated which can be great for more consistent results, but our relationships should not fall into mechanical monotony. Start by being mindful of your relationships with the people close to you and try to understand them. In addition to that, you should also be mindful of your purpose in life. A good way to do that is to have a set of short-term and long-term goals. These will make you more mindful of the things you do on a daily basis. Moreover, the practice of mindfulness can also be useful in other areas such as food and exercise.

Being mindful can also be about getting in touch with your brain. The best way to do it is to introduce daily meditation strategies. Meditation is the gateway to your mind; it will bring you more serenity and inner harmony. It will boost your consciousness and make you more aware of your surroundings as well as the things that happen around you. As a result, meditation will help you achieve a higher state of mind that is incredibly efficient at reducing stress.

Mindful meditation is a good way to start or end the day because it helps you become more in touch with your thoughts and feelings. You don't try to control your thoughts; you just observe them and take note of the patterns. In addition to that, it can be practiced anywhere as long as there is a calm and peaceful space. You don't need to rush or try harder because it's not about that.

Putting technology in its place

Recent technology is one of the greatest tools we can have access to. While using it to a certain extent can be beneficial, the issue arises when we get to the point where it starts controlling us. This calls for redefining it simply as a means to an end. Computers, phones, tablets, and any other devices are supposed to help us be more productive and more efficient.

However, the way technology has become such a ubiquitous part of our daily routine is undoubtedly negatively impacting our lives. So, it's very important that we establish new borders and rules for tech time. A good way to start is to limit watch time on your phone, only use it at a certain time, or even make your computer exclusive to work-related purposes. This will go a long way in making you more goal-driven in everyday life.

Prioritize sleep

Sleep is the single most underrated element of a healthy daily routine. It's the only time we get to rest, recharge, and regenerate. In addition to that, it's essential for our circadian rhythm. This is the cycle of the day, otherwise known as the biological clock, which can make us more energized in the morning and more relaxed at night.

By controlling the way we use technology, we also benefit from eliminating blue light, which is also known for negatively impacting our sleep.

"The problem is exacerbated by how technology affects teenagers. Teens sleeping with their iPhones and staying up all night texting are staples of our brave new digital world."

- Arianna Huffington, The Sleep Revolution: Transforming Your Life, One Night at a Time

It's important to set up a daily night routine for better sleep hygiene where you cut off any watch time two hours before sleep, and you ensure that there is no light source coming in. Your space should also be calmer and slightly more atmospheric for the perfect sleep environment.

By helping us keep the world in perspective, sleep gives us a chance to refocus on the essence of who we are. And in that place of connection, it is easier for the fears and concerns of the world to drop away.

- *Arianna Huffington, The Sleep Revolution: Transforming Your Life, One Night at a Time*

Your daily routines define how your day unfolds. They act as a checkpoint to make sure that you are on the right track. By setting a few daily habits and routines, you are ensuring that your day is more productive. Being mindful and practicing meditation can help a lot by allowing you to get in touch with your mind. In addition to that, you should also use technology for what it is, a convenience, and not let it ruin your precious moments or mess with vital aspects of your life, especially sleep: because, that's when you rest, regenerate, and prepare for another productive day.

A daily routine can help bring more structure and discipline into your life. It can also help you stay accountable and maintain your progress over time. But sometimes, even the most inspiring people can feel stuck in a rut, unable to make the next move -or any move for that matter.

Feeling deeply uninspired and unmotivated is completely normal. Letting yourself go can be an opportunity to take a step back and reevaluate your decisions. It's also the ideal opportunity to heed the wisdom of your body, encouraging you to slow down.

How to Stay Motivated and Stick with Your Goals

The fact is, we all have our moments of doubt, languidness, and utter disinterest. However, what sets successful people apart is their ability to channel their sense of determination and willpower, especially during tough times. With that said, staying focused on what lies ahead can be a daunting task.

The digital world is full of distractions. Instantaneous web access and constant texting don't make it any easier either. So how do you not give in to what seems easier at the moment? How do you maintain your motivation and stay on track?

Adopt a Dedicated Attitude and Mentality

In order for you to stay motivated, you have to first work on your attitude and mentality. There are two types of motivation: positive and negative. Positive motivation means you're more driven by the rewards of completing a given task.

On the other hand, negative motivation is when you focus on what will happen if you don't achieve that goal. If you're quick to jump to the worst-case scenario, that only sets you up for additional anxiety, stress, and frustration. When you're too focused on the negative outcomes, it's hard to stay determined and resilient.

However, when you shift your mindset from a state of desperation to one of enthusiasm and excitement, you will begin to see the benefits. Don't contemplate what you stand to lose from failing but rather what you stand to gain from succeeding. So picture your goal, channel your passion, and take action.

Whenever you're on the verge of spiralling down into those unproductive thoughts, choose a positive affirmation, and repeat it to yourself. The act of reiterating phrases like "I believe in myself" or "I am capable of whatever I set my mind to" reinforces that sense of determination.

Remind Yourself of Your WHY

If you have a set of goals or tasks to accomplish, then you must be aware of your 'why'. This is the thing that gets you out of bed despite how exhausted you are. It's what keeps you going no matter how many obstacles you face. It's also what drives you to work hard and be the best version of yourself that you can possibly be.

Knowing your "why" is essential when you want to get and stay motivated. Not only does it instill you with a sense of purpose, but it also creates necessity. Creating necessity stems from knowing why or for whom you want to achieve your goals and pursue your dreams.

You can't set a goal or a plan to reach that goal without knowing the reasoning behind this venture. So, whenever you catch yourself faltering or contemplating giving up, remind yourself of "why" you're doing this.

Keep in mind that your 'why' needs to be big enough to drive you to take action. If you haven't figured that out yet, it's time to dig deeper and embark on an insightful self-exploration odyssey.

Recondition Your Self-Talk

The way you talk to yourself internally directly influences your determination and motivation. The brain believes what you tell it most. So, how do you talk to yourself? Does it sound like this:

I have horrible luck

I'm not very creative

I'm no good at . . .

Things never work out for me

I'm terrible with people

If any of these phrases sound familiar to you, then you might be holding on to negative self-truths. These truths aren't necessarily accurate or representative of who you are as a person but rather stem from what you've been conditioned to believe.

If that's the case, then you need to reframe the way you talk to yourself. Not only are self-limiting beliefs tremendously unproductive and discouraging, but they hold no value. They will only set you far back on your path to success.

While letting go of these motivation buzzkills takes time and practice, you have to try. Committing to change is the hardest part, but it can be incredibly rewarding.

Motivation and productivity go hand in hand. If you want to achieve more, you need to take a closer look at your attitude, mindset, self-talk, and daily habits. In addition to that, you need to keep a constant reminder of your 'why' within reach. So when you stumble, it can act as your safety net. Then you bounce back, rediscover your purpose, and stride towards greatness.

Does Your Daily Routine Have Enough Downtime?

While seeking to increase your productivity and implement more positive habits that will push you to work on accomplishing your goals, you should also learn to listen to your mind and body's cues when they tell you to slow down. You might think that success requires working endless hours and sacrificing your sanity, but downtime is just as highly valued as being productive when it comes to your health and your ability to persevere.

We've all pondered over the habits of successful people, the things they do that make them successful in the first place. We've also been guilty of believing they work non-stop. Surely, they couldn't have gotten to where they are today if they weren't some variation of modern-day caffeinated workaholics.

Our very idea of what constitutes a productive day is deeply flawed because we associate it with working every minute of the day until we fall asleep, then wake up the next day and repeat. This pattern of overworking ourselves to the point of exhaustion is far from ideal.

In fact, it should be the opposite outcome we're looking for or seeking to achieve. Yet, we villainize downtime. We think any time not spent working is a wasted opportunity. We could have achieved more success, accomplished more goals, completed more tasks, . . . only if we kept working.

Do you see the issue here? Our daily routines have gradually morphed into this elaborate schedule filled to the brim with commitments, appointments, meetings, and obligations, to the extent that any 'free' time we dedicate to taking care of ourselves is considered to be a luxury, an indulgence on our part.

So, if you have to ask yourself if your routine has enough downtime, then you probably need more downtime.

Why Is Downtime Important?

Creating space for more free time can drastically improve your productivity and give you a much-needed energy boost. Heavy workloads and endless to-do lists can easily make us think we have no time for days off and vacations. With that said, driving too hard is bound to make us feel burned out, frustrated, and exhausted, which means we're not as efficient nor productive. When we're overexerting our physical and mental capacities, we're also less focused.

"Having free hours where I could relax and decompress made it possible for me to be effective during the working hours that remained. You need to value your free time, downtime, and leisurely activities that provide whole health and wellness to your life." — James Clear

Scheduling downtime into your daily routine will allow you to restore your focus, renew your energy levels, and rejuvenate your enthusiasm. Taking the time to step back and relax can also help you see the bigger picture, evaluate your priorities, and understand the purpose of every task you aim to accomplish. Not only that but downtime can also boost your mental and physical health as well as your interpersonal relationships. When you take time off and unplug, you also become better at listening to your mind and body. Ultimately, this will help you build a better relationship with yourself. Moreover, frequent breaks can reinstate your willpower, enhance your judgment, and encourage sound decision-making.

PUT IT INTO ACTION:

How can you better use your downtime?

When you recover or discover something that nourishes your soul and brings joy, care enough about yourself to make room for it in your life.

- *Jean Shinoda Bolen*

Schedule downtime into your day

If you're not naturally inclined to take breaks or slow down during the day, then you need to start scheduling downtime into your routine. Just as you would plan work activities and tasks, do the same for your free time. Whether it's an hour every day, one to two off days a week, or a couple of evenings here and there, it's essential that you allocate enough time for yourself where you get to unplug and relax.

Create rituals and routines

Routines and rituals are highly recommended habits for a healthy lifestyle. Scientists recommend creating routines that help you prepare for your day or unwind after work. This is a way to signal to your brain that it's time to start work, leave work, relax, meditate, or engage with your family and loved ones.

Free up your mind clutter

When you're taking downtime, you need to ensure that your mind is clutter-free. The purpose of downtime is to relax and unwind, so it defeats the purpose if you were to worry about work during your free time. Compartmentalizing tasks and responsibilities is a great way to do that. Organizing your daily to-do list so it's more comprehensible and less vague or messy also helps tremendously.

Self-care is not a waste of time; self-care makes your use of time more sustainable.

- Jackie Viramontez

While carving out space for downtime isn't always the easiest task, it's essential that you do so if you want to avoid burnout and chronic fatigue. Just as it's necessary to give your undivided attention to the tasks at hand, whether at work or at home, you also need to be able to enjoy your time off and focus on the present moment.

CHAPTER SIX RECAP:

Your ability to push through those walls and run those obstacles over will set you apart and set you up for success. Little tweaks in your daily routine can go a long way when it comes to building better habits and becoming more productive.

Three Daily Routines for Building a Better You:

1: Mindfulness practices & daily meditation strategies

2: Putting technology in its place

3: Prioritize sleep

How to Stay Motivated and Stick with Your Goals:

1: Adopt a dedicated attitude and mentality

2: Remind yourself of your WHY

3: Recondition your self-talk

Reminder: Schedule downtime into your day to give your body and mind time to rest.

Notes

Folks are usually about as happy as they make their minds up to be.

- Abraham Lincoln

You will never be happy if you continue to search for what happiness consists of. You will never live if you are looking for the meaning of life.

- Albert Camus

Happiness is when what you think, what you say, and what you do are in harmony.

- Mahatma Gandhi

CREATE A HAPPIER LIFE

What is happiness? How can we reach it? And once we do, will we be able to maintain it? These are all questions that have consumed spiritual leaders, philosophers, psychologists, and scientists alike. The same questions have attracted a growing number of neurologists over the last couple of decades, and their findings have revolutionized the way we perceive this emotion, not just in the field of psychology but also in the way many of us have been trying to cultivate happiness.

But the truth is, the relentless pursuit of happiness can often have the opposite effect and lead individuals to a more egoistic and self-centred lifestyle. However, this is a lonely pursuit only when its focal point is to generate positive feelings regardless of how it impacts other people. As Christopher McCandless, author of Into the Wild puts it, "Happiness [is] only real when [it's] shared." In this chapter, we will explore the three essential components of happiness, how your genetic composition can affect your happiness, the neuroscience behind this fascinating concept, as well as the four essential practices of happiness.

The Three Essential Components of Happiness

A study by Sonja Lyubomirsky and Kennon M. Sheldon on the pursuit of happiness defined it in terms of high life satisfaction, frequent positive circumstances, and infrequent negative ones. These constructs are what constitute subjective well-being or chronic happiness levels. Chronic happiness defines the levels of happiness over an extended period of time and not at one particular moment or day. In this regard, there are three primary factors influencing chronic happiness levels.

Life satisfaction

Life satisfaction is usually linked to positive emotions based on your past, present, and projections of future experiences. Your past can influence your future life satisfaction depending on how you frame that future in your mind. One pertinent example is thinking of the future in retrospect with past trauma, and as a result, you're trapped in a cycle of anticipating worst-case scenarios.

Meaning and purpose in life

Living a life of purpose and meaning, having goals and aspirations, and helping others through what you do can bring great feelings of satisfaction. When you don't have a clear sense of purpose that guides your thoughts and actions, you're likely to feel less focused, less efficient, but also more stressed because you don't feel aligned with the things you do.

Feeling engaged in what you do

Whether it's the work you do, the relationships you cultivate, or the way you spend your free time, feeling engaged with what you do on a daily basis is essential. The more invested you are in your career, hobbies, and the people you spend time with, the happier you are likely to be.

Do Your Genes Determine Your Happiness?

A 2016 study, "Happiness in Behaviour Genetics: An Update on Heritability and Changeability," found that genetic makeup is responsible for 32 to 40% of one's ability to be happy. The rest comes down to lifestyle along with other environmental factors. So, how do your genes determine your levels of happiness? And what are the other factors that come into play?

How Your Genes Affect Your Levels of Happiness

Early studies on the genetics of happiness were mainly conducted on twins and twins reared apart. The main question guiding these studies is one, perhaps as old as human history, the "nature vs nurture" debate. These studies focused on whether it is one's upbringing that makes them happy or whether their genes determine it.

Surprisingly, the findings concluded that there is a very high concordance between identical twins raised apart, but not so much for siblings in the same environment. It seemed that nature was playing a larger role than a shared environment.

When they looked back at serotonin receptors, dopamine, and other contributors to this emotion, then at the personality traits that are partly dependent on them, they found that people who are chronically happier are often extroverted and agreeable.

They also get large amounts of pleasure from their social lives, and they're somewhat dominant. All of these genes can, in a way, help them start off their lives a little happier than other individuals. Moreover, some of the other negative emotions (anger, sadness, fear, and lack of confidence) are not so pronounced in them.

On the other hand, some people are born more fearful and are more likely to be worrywarts. However, what is interesting is that these traits do not dictate the chronic emotional state of these people. So, although we are born with biological propensities, everyone can raise their happiness set point.

While research indicates that we are able to inherit positive traits like optimism, happiness, and self-esteem, a predisposition to a satisfying life is not the only aspect of happiness. Despite our genetic makeup, there are many ways in which we can learn how to be happier, no matter how challenging life can get. One way is by cultivating emotional resiliency and letting go of our perfectionist tendencies.

Can Science Make You Happier?

Happiness is a concept that has fascinated philosophers, theologians, neuroscientists, and cultural commentators for ages. Wanting to be happy is deeply anchored in human nature, and this has been a human pursuit for thousands of years. With that said, people know very little about the neuroscience behind this emotion.

Despite the expansive body of research and literature, scientists are only just beginning to truly grasp how the brain processes emotion and the chemical mechanism of how this impacts our thoughts and behaviour.

In the past couple of decades, positive psychology has taken this notion into the realm of scientific and academic research to gain deeper insight into meaningful living and well-being. So, how do scientists explain happiness, and can science and technological advancements make you happier?

The Science of Happiness

As scientists are working to better understand the brain, human DNA, and the science of how personality develops and is constrained, they're looking to get a more precise idea of not only what happiness looks like now but how it can be tweaked as well.

This will allow scientists to better understand how they can help people by looking at their brains managing their self-talk. For many individuals, this will require small tweaks in behaviour and action that will greatly impact their levels of happiness.

People always think that to be happy, they have to encounter or acquire something big and phenomenal. They think, "If only I got that job promotion," "If only I got that house," "If only I got that bonus" . . . then I will be happy. But happiness mainly accrues from our attitudes and our thoughts and very slow but important daily changes.

What Causes Happiness?

Your happiness depends on numerous variables. Your emotional state fluctuates according to how you react to changes in your personal life, finances, career, and relationships. Happiness can also be the end result of engaging in acts of kindness and giving back to your community. Not only that, but happiness is also due in part to you adopting a growth and abundant mindset that allows you to make progress in life, especially during challenging times.

With that said, there is another aspect of happiness, which is the neuroscience behind it. Neurological chemicals such as serotonin and dopamine vary from one person to the next, which causes them to feel more or less happy and satisfied with themselves and the lives they lead.

Because we're wired to pursue pleasure and avoid pain, we often look not only to survive but to seek experiences that make us happy and fulfilled. Our brain chemistry is designed to sustain these efforts by releasing happy-feeling chemicals into our bodies and brains.

Serotonin, for instance, is produced in the brain and intestines. This neurotransmitter is circulated in the bloodstream and across the central nervous system. While it's connected to blood clotting, digestion, and bone density, serotonin is most importantly known for its mood-regulating function.

Scientists refer to this neurotransmitter as the "happiness chemical" since higher serotonin levels work to increase confidence and feelings of well-being and belonging. So, people with significant serotonin levels often report being happier, while people struggling with depression show lower levels of this chemical.

Although there are many pills and medications that target regulating serotonin levels, a 2018 study ("Successfully Striving for Happiness") shows that pursuing happiness through social means is more effective than other methods. This includes spending more time with family and friends, considering how serotonin is more free-flowing when a person feels seen, heard, and valued by their close social circle.

Is There a Secret to a Happier Life?

Happiness is one of the most significant dimensions of the human experience, in part because it yields a plethora of rewards both for the individual and for society as a whole. In recent years, many countries around the world, namely Canada, France, and Britain, have implemented a citizen happiness index as a key indicator of the nation's prosperity in their official national statistics.

But what are the decisive factors that contribute to this emotion, and how can we identify, gauge, and employ them to improve the quality of our lives? How can we contribute to our happiness but also to that of the people around us? Most importantly, is there a secret to leading a happier life?

Cortisol: The Enemy of Happiness

There are many biological conditions that can decrease the levels of serotonin and dopamine. However, these chemicals are typically balanced in individuals who eat balanced diets, get regular physical activity, and are able to manage their stress levels.

On the other hand, people who lead unhealthy lifestyles often allow stress to take over in the form of a dangerous chemical called cortisol. This hormone, produced by the body's adrenal glands, can inhibit the neurotransmitters responsible for our levels of chronic happiness.

In normal amounts, cortisol can reduce inflammation, regulate blood sugar and blood pressure, as well as promote healthy sleep cycles. On the other hand, cortisol levels spike when you're living in a constant state of stress and anxiety.

This not only reduces your dopamine and serotonin production but also negatively impacts your focus, productivity, and memory. As a result, this can have nefarious repercussions on major organs as well as the immune system.

In simpler terms, dopamine and serotonin make you happy, but you can't experience the positive only at all times. Your body needs both and ultimately, what generates happiness all comes down to one thing, that is balance.

Can We Learn to Be Happier? 4 Ways to Practice Happiness

You may believe that because your brain is wired a certain way, there is very little you can do to bring more balance and happiness into your life. After all, part of this is all about genetics, right? While it's true that your biology does dictate your brain chemistry, the science of happiness and positive psychology shows that you have the power to transform your mindset and change your thoughts. Here is the fundamental practice for a happier life.

Bring your mind into the present

In a recent study conducted by psychologists, Matthew A. Killingsworth and Daniel T. Gilbert said, "A Wandering Mind Is an Unhappy Mind," and found adults spend an average of 50% of their time in the present moment.

The scientists also compiled data on chronic happiness levels and found that we tend to be at our happiest when we are in the present moment, regardless of what it is that we're doing. The reason behind this is that when we're more present and in the moment, we fully experience our surroundings.

Instead of getting caught up in an overwhelming race to accomplish things faster, we slow down, allowing ourselves to be fully engaged in our endeavours. While undoing a habit you've had for years may not be the easiest task, it all comes down to awareness.

So, whenever you notice your brain following future-oriented thoughts and ideas, choose not to follow that train of thought. Instead, give your mind a nudge towards the present. Try to reorient your focus on what is going on around you. It's no easy exercise, but with some practice, you can reinforce your ability to stay in the present.

Volunteer

According to a 2020 study ("Does Volunteering Make Us Happier or Are Happier People More Likely to Volunteer?") that examines the correlation between volunteering and well-being, when you do something for other people, this takes the attention away from yourself and can make you feel good. Before the 18th century, happiness has always been about living a virtuous life.

However, when people began to think of happiness as the manifestation of positive emotions and good feelings, this resulted in a profound shift. With the emergence of positive psychology, people have rediscovered the true value of virtues.

Moreover, studies show that when a person feels gratitude, kindness, forgiveness, and other virtues, they report higher levels of happiness and satisfaction. In this regard, practicing gratitude and kindness is one of the most powerful happiness inducers.

So, make a habit of doing loving, generous, and considerate things for others on a daily basis. Get involved with causes that inspire you to be better and share not just your money but also your time and energy. Even if you can't make a permanent commitment to volunteering, engage in random acts of kindness, no matter how small or insignificant they seem.

Move your body

Physical activity isn't just a way to maintain your body's fitness and flexibility, it's also essential for your mental health. Regular exercise has been proven to have therapeutic benefits* namely in alleviating psychiatric illnesses, promoting brain injury recovery, and preventing neurodegenerative diseases.

Dopamine, Serotonin, and Noradrenaline are three major neurotransmitters known to be modulated by physical activity. Movement helps release these happiness chemicals, and doctors recommend 150 minutes of moderate exercise per week, which breaks down to five days of 30-minute sessions.

Feed your mind

The thoughts you continuously feed your mind have a direct ef-

---

* https://www.ncbi.nlm.nih.gov/pmc/articles/PMC4061837/

fect on your levels of happiness and satisfaction. So naturally, if all you can bring yourself to focus on is the negative in every situation you encounter, frustration and resentment will entail.

On the other hand, if you make conscious efforts to consume positive content and find the silver lining in the darkest and most difficult of periods, you will feel more content, and by extension, build better emotional resiliency which is crucial in managing stress and navigating daily challenges. So, make a point of feeding your mind with valuable self-help books, inspiring podcasts, and positive stories.

Neuroscience shows that there is much more to happiness than your DNA or natural predisposition to optimism. By bringing your mind to the present moment, engaging in acts of kindness, practicing gratitude, and making progress in life, you have the power to reframe your mindset so it's more susceptible to experiencing positive emotions rather than dwelling in negative ones.

Your mindset matters, so shift your thinking

Scientific research suggests that each one of us has a happiness set point. One particular study on the relativity of happiness explored the example of winning the lottery versus suffering a spinal cord injury. The findings conclude that positive and negative events (even the most extreme) knock us off our baseline.

However, over time, we do tend to return to roughly the same set point of happiness, whether we're wealthy millionaires or whether we're confined to a wheelchair. This set point is mainly based on our genetics but also our fundamental belief system and the way we think. The thing about this system of beliefs we hold is that it begins to govern the way we think and behave; and, more often than not, the habits of thinking we develop are inaccurate.

For instance, if you think you're not as good as other people, then you will internalize that idea as a fact, and this 'fact' will constrict your perception of what you can and cannot do. With that said, when you gain a deeper understanding of these inaccurate beliefs and unfounded feelings, you can work on increasing your happiness baseline or set point.

The more you're able to detect the exaggerations for what they are, the less they will affect you. You can only do this by paying close attention to your emotional reflexes and responses to give yourself a chance to challenge the negative thoughts and self-limiting beliefs that underlie them.

The promising field of positive psychology has proven time and time again that the secret to happiness does not reside in turning your frown upside down, nor does it entail ignoring life's challenges and difficulties. It's not about forcing yourself to feel happy when you don't either.

Rather it's about taking proactive steps to shift the way you think and challenge your core attitudes and behaviours in a gradual manner. Is there an ultimate secret to finding more happiness? Not necessarily. It's a collective of efforts deployed on your part to confront your self-limiting beliefs and shift your mindset to continuous growth, development, and self-improvement.

While no one feels happy all the time, science shows that what causes happiness is in part due to our thoughts, behaviour, and action. Although there are biological factors that can decrease happiness chemicals, there are things we can do to boost this emotion. To answer the initial question, "Can science make you happier?" Yes, it can, but you also have the power to "rewire" your brain and redirect your thoughts from negative to positive (or at the very least a neutral state of being).

PUT IT INTO ACTION:

Create your own Happiness Practice

Day 1: Pick a notepad to become your Happiness Journal. Set your intention for the week and visualize how amazing your life will be on the last day of this week:

> I intend to have . . .
>
> I intend to be . . .
>
> I intend to do...
>
> . . . By the last day of this week
>
> Set a mantra for the week to repeat to yourself each morning.
>
> Examples:
>
> I CAN be truly happy.
>
> People LOVE to support me.
>
> I am truly deserving of being happy!

Day 2: Write down your reasons for being happy. Meditate on what you write down in your new Happiness Journal.

Day 3: Write down what you are grateful for today, this week, this year, in your life. Take time to re-read your list to yourself and sit with the emotions your gratitude list brings up.

Day 4: Create a "Happy Space." Clear a space for yourself to turn into a happy space. It can be a corner, a room, or your entire home—but carve out a space, clear as much clutter as you can, and fill it with small things that speak to you and make you happy.

Day 5: Visualize your happiest self. Sit or lay down in your happy space and close your eyes. In your mind's eye, step out of your body and look back. What does your happiest self look like? Step into yourself and feel all the happiness wash over you. Stay in your visualization for as long as you want, then count to five and open your eyes.

Day 6: Give joy to someone else. Donate money, bring someone a coffee, tip extra—find a way to give joy to someone today!

Day 7: Movement day! Take time to move your body today. Even if it's a short walk or a few jumping jacks, set time aside to deliberately move your body and get active. Think of it as a gift to yourself!

You can repeat this practice or shuffle the days—whatever makes you happiest!

CHAPTER SEVEN RECAP:

Happiness can be developed from a collective of efforts deployed on your part to confront your self-limiting beliefs and shift your mindset to continuous growth, development, and self-improvement.

Three Essential Components of Happiness

1: Life satisfaction

2: Meaning and purpose in life

3: Feeling engaged in what you do

This chapter will make you happy if you are interested in:

Genetics & Happiness

The Science of Happiness

Cortisol: The Enemy of Happiness

4 Ways to Practice Happiness

1: Bring your mind to the present

2: Volunteer

3: Move your body

4: Feed your mind

Notes

A leader takes people where they want to go. A great leader takes people where they don't necessarily want to go, but ought to be.

- Rosalynn Carter

The first responsibility of a leader is to define reality. The last is to say thank you. In between, the leader is a servant.

- Max DePree

If your actions inspire others to dream more, learn more, do more and become more, you are a leader.

- John Quincy Adams

FINDING YOUR PURPOSE AND GUIDING OTHERS ON THEIR OWN PATH

In this chapter, we delve into finding your purpose as a woman, and a leader. We also dig into the best instruments and tools to implement that will help you innovate but also guide others on their own paths to greatness.

Know Yourself

Leaders have a good sense of who they are, what is meaningful to them, and what they strive to accomplish. A successful leader knows their purpose in life and work.

If you want to inspire others and push them toward more growth, first, you need to cultivate a deep sense of purpose that incites them to be the best version of themselves.

Articulate your vision

The foundation of any successful individual, business, or company is the mission they're working towards and the vision they stand to achieve. This includes what they do well and where they're headed. This vision needs to be as specific as possible, it cannot be vague, and as a leader, you have to be able to articulate it in a clear and concise manner so that if you're leading a team, others are inspired to collaborate and work together toward a common goal.

SMART GOALS

For your goals to be impactful, they need to adhere to the S-M-A-R-T goal strategy. This approach is designed to help you set goals that you and your team members are bound to achieve. So, if you're unsure about your goal-setting abilities, follow the SMART design. This acronym stands for:

Specific: Beyond writing them down, you need to envision them in your head with a great deal of precision and clarity. You have to put yourself in that headspace as if the goal you have has already been achieved. Moreover, you need to write down what every aspect of your life will be like. Your goals need to be well-thought, well-formulated, and well-defined. This not only gives you a better image of the future you're planning, but it also provides you with a sense of direction. So, in this way, your goals will show you the way and how you can get to where you want to be.

Measurable: Beyond being specific, your goals also need to be measurable. You have to be able to track your progress, and the only way to do that is through a metric that you can keep up with. Include precise amounts, dates, figures, and so on. For instance, you can easily track your money goals if you have a specific number you strive to reach. Don't just state that you will reduce expenses because you won't be able to know if you've been successful. It could be a projected percentage that you intend to hit in one month's time or within the next two years.

Attainable: There's a misconception that setting attainable goals or realistic goals means you have to limit yourself to only the things you can achieve. However, setting attainable goals doesn't mean you can't think beyond the scope of what you've been able to achieve so far. The key element here is finding the perfect balance between realistic and challenging. If you set a goal that you have no hope of achieving, this will only feel discouraging. On the other hand, if you set a goal that is too easy, this will only make you fearful of setting bigger or riskier goals. Work on setting attainable goals that incite you to raise the bar and challenge yourself because those bring the most personal satisfaction and fulfillment.

Relevant: This step helps you ensure that whatever goals you set matter to you. They are relevant to the direction you intend. In addition to that, they should also line up with other relevant goals. If you set conflicting or inconsistent goals, not only will you waste your time chasing outcomes of no consequence, but you also set yourself up for failure. A relevant goal should have a positive answer to the following questions:

Does this feel worthwhile?

Is it the right time to pursue this?

Does this align with my needs?

Am I the right person to do this?

Is it applicable at this stage of my life?

Time-bound: Goal setting is pointless if you don't have a precise time frame in mind. It's all about having a set deadline, down to the day, month, and year. Having a date set gives you a great incentive to work that much harder towards achieving your goals. Not only that, but it allows you to break down one big goal into smaller ones. Hitting those milestones will help you feel more confident and accomplished. Moreover, it also makes that ultimate goal a lot more manageable. Nothing is out of bounds as long as you follow through every day, building momentum, doing little by little, accomplishing one thing at a time. This is how you set yourself up for long-term success.

IF YOU'RE LEADING A TEAM...

Help your team members grow

Leaders make a daily commitment to the people who work for and with them. They give their employees ample room for self-expression, and they help them develop their own skills and talents.

Often, a leader can be intimidating when considering the power they hold, but a successful leader knows how to deflect the attention away from themselves and encourage others to voice their opinions.

They're also great communicators and are able to remind everyone of the expectations they have for the team. If you are serious about being a successful leader, you have to make an effort to understand the mindset and perception of each member of the group.

Communication that may work with one person may be completely ineffective for the next. So you have to be able to identify the most efficient techniques to challenge each and every person in the team to grow, evolve, and excel.

Managing other people is a daunting task, to say the least, but beyond mentoring and sponsoring employees, you also need to be accountable to others and show them that their success matters to you too!

Encourage innovation and embrace new ideas

The business climate and landscape are always changing, so in order for your enterprise to succeed and stay on top of the trends, you have to be open to new ideas, encourage innovation, and incite others to think outside of the box.

You also need to showcase your flexibility and ability to adapt and take risks in good times and bad times. Moreover, as a leader, you have to be prepared to unearth opportunities—as peculiar as they might be—to launch new initiatives, new strategies, but also improve already existing products and services.

Continuous improvement is imperative to the success of your company and the people in it. Challenging your team and pushing them to reach for more will help you create a positive and inspiring company culture. This is how you set the tone, lead by example, and bring to the workplace an attitude that motivates your employees to take action.

Be a great teacher but also a great student

More often than not, at one point in time, employees will tell you that their leaders have stopped performing their roles as mentors and teachers. This could be because they're more focused on other aspects of the business or simply because they don't think they have anything more to teach.

While the first may hold some truth, the latter doesn't. Successful leaders never stop learning; they're constantly seeking new opportunities, new knowledge, and new ways to educate themselves, so by extension, they always have something exciting or groundbreaking to share, if not some tidbits of wisdom, judgment, and experience.

If you look up the many habits of successful people, you will find "a drive to self-improve and learn" to be one of the leading routines. The truth is, outstanding leaders make sure to dedicate some time in their day entirely to reading or listening to audiobooks and podcasts.

If you think about it, there's always something new to learn, and there's always room for growth and expansion. Successful leaders are great teachers, but they're even greater students. They keep themselves well-informed of the latest trends, but they also actively work on imparting that same knowledge to their team members.

To conclude this chapter, once you begin to implement these notions into how you're leading others, you will soon create a new paradigm defined by growth and accomplishment. And when you realize that your purpose as a leader holds immense power in the meaningful impact you can create, you will gain a better understanding of how you can best serve others, all while sustaining your successes and increasing the value of your organization's brand.

CHAPTER EIGHT RECAP:

Know Yourself

Develop a sense of who you are, what is meaningful to you, and what you strive to accomplish.

Articulate Your Vision

The foundation of success is the mission it's working towards and the vision it stands to achieve.

SMART goals

Create goals that are specific, measurable, attainable, relevant, and time-bound, a.k.a. SMART.

Help your team members grow

Leaders make a daily commitment to the people who work for and with them.

Encourage innovation and embrace new ideas

It's important to be open to new ideas, encourage innovation, and incite others to think outside of the box.

Be a great teacher but also a great student

There is always something new to learn, and there's always room for growth and expansion.

Notes

FINAL TAKEAWAY PROJECT

Now that you are ready and prepared to love and lead from the heart and be you, unapologetically, I have a final assignment for you to launch yourself towards even more success in your authenticity journey. But first... take some time to go back, reflect on the takeaway from each chapter – or, if you missed any, take the next 30 days to try them out! If you didn't complete each "Put It Into Action" section, don't fret – there is still time! This book is a resource for you to access any time you want to brush up on your ability to just be who you are and revisit ways to implement living authentically.

Imagine Yourself 30 Days Later...

It takes 21-28 days to form a habit, so the next month is your opportunity to grow into your authentic, empowered lifestyle. We covered affirmations, thought experiments, alignment, strategic downtime planning, and prioritizing happiness – so let's dive into those toolboxes and create a sustainable recurring practice that you can use to harness your new abilities and step into the best you! Bring out the journal you've been using to complete the takeaways or grab a blank journal [is there anything more exciting than a blank journal?] and get ready to immerse yourself in this wonderful journey of living in your strength.

28-DAY FINAL TAKEAWAY PROJECT

Create your own BE YOU UNAPOLOGETICALLY routine:

START:

At the end of these 28 days,

I will have…

I will be…

I will feel…

Week 1:

Daily Affirmation(s): [see chapter one]

Value focus: [see chapter four]

Scheduled downtime: [see chapter six]

Week 2:

Daily Affirmation(s): [see chapter one]

Reasons for being happy this week: [see chapter seven]

Scheduled downtime: [see chapter six]

Week 3:

Daily Affirmation(s): [see chapter one]

Value focus: [see chapter four]

Scheduled downtime: [see chapter six]

Week 4:

Daily Affirmation(s): [see chapter one]

Reasons for being happy this week: [see chapter seven]

Scheduled downtime: [see chapter six]

END

Reflect on the following items using a 1-10 scale (1 being the worst and 10 being the best); your energy, happiness levels, relationships, internal self-talk – what has changed, how do you feel? [Tip: writing it down will help reinforce the habit!]

Final affirmation:

Now that these 28 days are complete, I plan to continue living authentically and to be me, unapologetically!

Repeat this practice as many times as you like – revisit this process every three months or when you need a refresher!

CONCLUSION

When you first decided to read this book, you were probably looking for better ways to be assertive and express yourself as a leader, rather than going on a self-discovery trip and learning all about your emotional and mental fitness. Perhaps it was more in-depth in that regard than what you would have expected.

That is the main reason I felt compelled to develop the chapters in this book. From realizing your emotional resilience and building a better you through habits of success, to finding your purpose as a woman, and leader, I am driven to support you in your journey and in guiding others on their own paths to self-development and success.

Throughout the pages of this book, we discussed all the mindset myths that have been holding you back from unlocking your full potential. We delved deep into the beliefs we hold about ourselves and how those control our lives but also the way we see the world.

We learned how our negative self-talk inhibits our abilities and puts us in a stuck headspace from which we can't detach ourselves. We addressed the many aspects of building confidence, speaking our truth, living honest to our values, and setting goals that align with our principles.

I truly hope I helped lessen the weight on your shoulders that you've been holding, or at the very least get rid of some of the pieces of your armour suit that you've been wearing each time you get out of your comfort zone.

I also hope you better understand your own responsibilities in retrospect to those of the people around you. I know it took me a while before I began to accept the fact that some things simply aren't within my control. In the same way, I want you to take that insight with you on whatever path you venture out into next.

Remember to always seek to improve the things you can, but also trust yourself to let go of trying to control the things you can't. True happiness only happens when we embark on our journey toward self-acceptance, compassion, and empathy.

You know better than resisting your thoughts and feelings. You also know better than to passively accept whatever is happening around you. As you grow and move on, you don't have to feel obligated to 'conquer' your anxiety in that sense, nor do you have to endure it with rigid force.

It all comes down to what steps you choose to take. So, make the most of your life. Make it something grand and monumental, something that is much bigger than your worries and fears. There's no going back, no way to regain the lost moments of the past.

Stay focused on what is ahead of you and make your values a reality. You already have the skills; you just need to nurture them. Get out of your mind, be bold, be brave, and make the daily commitment to honour your true self!

ACKNOWLEDGEMENTS

I wrote this book in the hope that it would help leaders unlock their full potential, find their purpose, and cultivate the confidence they need to lead from the heart. I am beyond grateful to have had such a strong, encouraging, and inspiring support system guiding me every step of the long—sometimes rocky road from the early stages of this book to its release. I truly couldn't have done it alone. I am privileged to have them in my life.

There is nothing that brings me more joy, happiness, and fulfillment in the world than guiding others on their own paths to success. Though now, it is my turn to give credit where credit is due and thank the countless people who have been involved in the process of bringing this book to life.

This has been a dream of mine for so long that I can hardly believe it's come to fruition and is complete. I simply couldn't have done it without the immense help and support of the following two people: Shelly Lynn Hughes and Khaoula. You have touched my life in so many ways and I can't thank you enough for the excitement, passion, and support you bring into my world. You're both such amazing women.

Writing a book, while much more challenging than I anticipated, is certainly incredibly rewarding. This wouldn't have been possible without Khaoula's insightful contributions and expertise.

I'm eternally grateful to you, Shelly, and the amazing team at Fresh Magazine for all the support you have shown me on this life-changing journey. I appreciate the trust you all have put in me as well as the time and energy you have invested in my project. Working with you has been a true privilege and I feel so blessed to have gotten this chance.

Andreia, your patience, your scrupulous attention to detail, your commitment to excellence, and your unwavering dedication have been indispensable throughout this process. It is because of your constant guidance, your monumental efforts, and your auspicious encouragement that I can now call myself an author. I am forever indebted to you!

Laura, you have believed in me since day one, and I wouldn't be where I am or who I am today without you by my side! Thank you from the bottom of my heart for all your love and support throughout the years.

To my late dad, Fred, who has always encouraged me to be authentically myself and to pursue my dreams, and to my mom, Heather, who showed me the importance of lifelong learning, I love you both, unconditionally. I am forever grateful for all the valuable lessons you have taught me.

Mom, thank you for being my biggest fan and inspiration throughout my life. I admire your kindness, strength, positivity, and resilience. You are a wonderful woman, and I am proud to call you, my mom. I truly wouldn't have achieved such success if not for your always-present love and support.

To my amazing husband, Carlos, thank you for being my love, spouse, best friend, soulmate, and more. I am the luckiest wife to have such a wonderful, understanding, and appreciative partner. Thank you for all the things you do to make me the happiest woman in the world and thank you for always cheering me on in all my entrepreneurial pursuits. We have been through it all and I continually look forward to our future endeavours. I love you more than I can put into words.

To my sweet, dear three kids, Jacob, Jaden, and Jordan who always remind me of the great value the little things in life hold. I believe in YOU all, and I cannot wait to see how far you will go in life. You're the best thing that ever happened to me and I am so grateful to have you call me mom/ (Jordan—step Momma).

I am indebted to my recent mentor, Michelle Cunningham, who has been invaluable to my growth, both personally and professionally. You have shaped my life in a profound way when I stepped out of a professional career that was familiar to embrace entrepreneurship, the unknown, and social media—my biggest fear (wink); so, thank you for being such an integral part of my success. You breathed belief into me at the onset when I took your course, and that belief has never wavered.

I would like to thank the many people who reviewed the initial drafts of this book and provided their valuable feedback, including, Dr. Divi Chandna, Lorna Vanderhaeghe, and Alyson Jones. You women motivate me to continually be my best self. I adore and love you all!

And finally, to you, the reader. Thank you for taking the time to read this book. I hope it brings you the level of clarity and fulfillment you need to pursue the dream life you deserve!

MORE RESOURCES

Affirmations:

I trust the Universe. It gives me exactly what I need at exactly the right time.

Everything works out perfectly for me. I am creating my dream life.

I am worthy of receiving. Now release everything that is not serving my highest purpose.

I'm worthy enough to follow my dreams and manifest my desires.

My business gets better and better every day.

I work where I want, when I want, and with people I want to work with.

I am abundant in my finances, in happiness, and in love.

My soul is ready to live the life of my dreams.

I am wealthy and prosperous in every aspect of my life.

I surround myself with positive and genuine people who help

me and encourage me to reach my goals.

The Universe always has my back.

I now release any fears or limiting beliefs I may have about achieving my best.

Every day I am moving toward my best life.

I am smart, creative, and motivated. I only take yes for an answer.

My intentions for my life are clear. What I am seeking is seeking me.

It is OK for me to have everything I want. Every day I move towards having everything I want.

I'm creating a life of passion and purpose.

I step out of my comfort zone to achieve my goals and find comfort in change and new environments.

I love, support, and believe in myself.

There is no place for negative self-talk in my life. I am completely and utterly in love with myself.

ABOUT THE AUTHOR

Amanda Da Silva is an educator by profession, an entrepreneur by nature, and a two-time Amazon-Best-Selling Co-author of Pursuit:365. Formerly the CEO of a K-12 Independent School in Vancouver, B.C., Amanda is a passionate and consummate professional. She holds a bachelor's degree in both Human Kinetics and Education, and a master's degree in Leadership and Administration.

With a calling to empower the people around her with purpose and authenticity, Amanda has expanded her role as an educator and become an industry thought leader in confidence coaching. She has over twenty years of experience in the education and business sectors to pull from and is now sharing her curated knowledge with wider audiences through her writing and one-on-one coaching.

Expanding her classroom to a global audience, in 2020, Amanda founded DS Education Group as well as her own personal development and leadership coaching brand. She continuously brings energy and excitement to lifelong learning for students and clients alike, providing a supportive educational community and unparalleled training courses and resources to enhance their future dreams and goals.

Find out more about Amanda on her personal website:

www.amanda-dasilva.com/about-me

CPSIA information can be obtained
at www.ICGtesting.com
Printed in the USA
LVHW021923220423
744619LV00002B/6